P9-CDP-351

English Men of Letters

EDITED BY JOHN MORLEY

CHAUCER

BY

ADOLPHUS WILLIAM WARD

NEW YORK

HARPER & BROTHERS, PUBLISHERS

FRANKLIN SQUARE

1880

NOTE.

THE peculiar conditions of this essay must be left to explain themselves. It could not have been written at all without the aid of the Publications of the Chaucer Society, and more especially of the labours of the Society's Director, Mr. Furnivall. To other recent writers on Chaucer—including Mr. Fleay, from whom I never differ but with hesitation—I have referred, in so far as it was in my power to do so. Perhaps I may take this opportunity of expressing a wish that Pauli's *History of England*, a work beyond the compliment of an acknowledgment, were accessible to every English reader.

A. W. W.

CONTENTS.

CHAUCER.

CHAPTER I.

CHAUCER'S TIMES.

THE biography of Geoffrey Chaucer is no longer a mixture
of unsifted facts, and of more or less hazardous conjectures. Many and wide as are the gaps in our knowledge
concerning the course of his outer life, and doubtful as
many important passages of it remain—in vexatious contrast with the certainty of other relatively insignificant
data—we have at least become aware of the foundations
on which alone a trustworthy account of it can be built.
These foundations consist partly of a meagre though gradually increasing array of external evidence, chiefly to be
found in public documents—in the Royal Wardrobe Book,
the Issue Rolls of the Exchequer, the Customs Rolls, and
such-like records—partly of the conclusions which may be
drawn with confidence from the internal evidence of the
poet's own indisputably genuine works, together with a
few references to him in the writings of his contemporaries
or immediate successors. Which of his works are to be
accepted as genuine, necessarily forms the subject of an
antecedent enquiry, such as cannot with any degree of

1*

safety be conducted except on principles far from infallible with regard to all the instances to which they have been applied, but now accepted by the large majority of competent scholars. Thus, by a process which is in truth dulness and dryness itself, except to patient endeavour stimulated by the enthusiasm of special literary research, a limited number of results has been safely established, and others have, at all events, been placed beyond reasonable doubt. Around a third series of conclusions or conjectures the tempest of controversy still rages; and even now it needs a wary step to pass without fruitless deviations through a maze of assumptions consecrated by their longevity, or commended to sympathy by the fervour of personal conviction.

A single instance must suffice to indicate both the difficulty and the significance of many of those questions of Chaucerian biography which, whether interesting or not in themselves, have to be determined before Chaucer's life can be written. They are not, "all and some," mere antiquarians' puzzles, of interest only to those who have leisure and inclination for microscopic enquiries. So with the point immediately in view. It has been said with much force that Tyrwhitt, whose services to the study of Chaucer remain uneclipsed by those of any other scholar, would have composed a quite different biography of the poet, had he not been confounded by the formerly (and here and there still) accepted date of Chaucer's birth, the year 1328. For the correctness of this date Tyrwhitt "supposed" the poet's tombstone in Westminster Abbey to be the voucher; but the slab placed on a pillar near his grave (it is said at the desire of Caxton) appears to have merely borne a Latin inscription without any dates; and the marble monument erected in its stead, "in the name of the Muses," by Nicolas Brigham in 1556, while giving October 25th, 1400, as the day of Chaucer's death, makes no mention either of the date of his birth or of the number of years to which he attained, and, indeed, promises no more information than it gives. That Chaucer's contemporary, the poet Gower, should have referred to him in the year 1392 as "now in his days old," is at best a very vague sort of testimony, more especially as it is by mere conjecture that the year of Gower's own birth is placed as far back as 1320. Still less weight can be attached to the circumstance that another poet, Occleve, who clearly regarded himself as the disciple of one by many years his senior, in accordance with the common phraseology of his (and, indeed, of other) times, spoke of the older writer as his "father" and "father reverent." In a coloured portrait carefully painted from memory by Occleve on the margin of a manuscript, Chaucer is represented with grey hair and beard; but this could not of itself be taken to contradict the supposition that he died about the age of sixty. And Leland's assertion that Chaucer attained to old age self-evidently rests on tradition only; for Leland was born more than a century after Chaucer died. Nothing occurring in any of Chaucer's own works of undisputed genuineness throws any real light on the subject. His poem, the *House of Fame*, has been variously dated; but at any period of his manhood he might have said, as he says there, that he was "too old" to learn astronomy, and preferred to take his science on faith. In the curious lines called *L'Envoy de Chaucer à Scogan*, the poet, while blaming his friend for his want of perseverance in a love-suit, classes himself among "them that be hoar and round of shape," and speaks of himself and his Muse as out of date and rusty. But there seems no sufficient reason for removing

the date of the composition of these lines to an earlier
year than 1393; and poets as well as other men since
Chaucer have spoken of themselves as old and obsolete at
fifty. A similar remark might be made concerning the
reference to the poet's old age, "which dulleth him in his
spirit," in the *Complaint of Venus*, generally ascribed to
the last decennium of Chaucer's life. If we reject the evidence of a further passage, in the *Cuckoo and the Night-
ingale*, a poem of disputed genuineness, we accordingly
arrive at the conclusion that there is no reason for demur-
ring to the only direct external evidence in existence as to
the date of Chaucer's birth. At a famous trial of a cause
of chivalry held at Westminster in 1386, Chaucer, who had
gone through part of a campaign with one of the litigants,
appeared as a witness; and on this occasion his age was,
doubtless on his own deposition, recorded as that of a
man " of forty years and upwards," who had borne arms
for twenty-seven years. A careful enquiry into the accuracy of the record as to the ages of the numerous other
witnesses at the same trial has established it in an over-
whelming majority of instances; and it is absurd gratuitously to charge Chaucer with having understated his age
from motives of vanity. The conclusion, therefore, seems
to remain unshaken, that he was born about the year 1340,
or some time between that year and 1345.

Now, we possess a charming poem by Chaucer called
the *Assembly of Fowls*, elaborately courtly in its conception, and in its execution giving proofs of Italian reading
on the part of its author, as well as of a ripe humour such
as is rarely an accompaniment of extreme youth. This
poem has been thought by earlier commentators to allego-
rise an event known to have happened in 1358; by later
critics, another which occurred in 1364. Clearly, the as-

sumption that the period from 1340 to 1345 includes the
date of Chaucer's birth suffices of itself to stamp the one
of these conjectures as untenable, and the other as improbable, and (when the style of the poem and treatment of
its subject are taken into account) adds weight to the other
reasons in favour of the date 1381 for the poem in question.   Thus, backwards and forwards, the disputed points
in Chaucer's biography and the question of his works are
affected by one another.

Chaucer's life, then, spans rather more than the latter
half of the fourteenth century, the last year of which was
indisputably the year of his death.   In other words, it
covers rather more than the interval between the most
glorious epoch of Edward III.'s reign — for Crecy was
fought in 1346 — and the downfall, in 1399, of his unfortunate successor Richard II.

The England of this period was but a little land, if
numbers be the test of greatness; but in Edward III.'s
time, as in that of Henry V., who inherited so much of
Edward's policy and revived so much of his glory, there
stirred in this little body a mighty heart.   It is only of a
small population that the author of the *Vision concerning
Piers Plowman* could have gathered the representatives
into a single field, or that Chaucer himself could have
composed a family picture fairly comprehending, though
not altogether exhausting, the chief national character-
types.   In the year of King Richard II.'s accession (1377),
according to a trustworthy calculation based upon the result of that year's poll-tax, the total number of the inhabitants of England seems to have been two millions and a

half. A quarter of a century earlier—in the days of Chaucer's boyhood—their numbers had been perhaps twice as
large. For not less than four great pestilences (in 1348–9,
1361–2, 1369, and 1375–6) had swept over the land, and at
least one-half of its population, including two-thirds of the
inhabitants of the capital, had been carried off by the ravages of the obstinate epidemic—"the foul death of England," as it was called in a formula of execration in use
among the people. In this year—1377—London, where
Chaucer was doubtless born as well as bred, where the
greater part of his life was spent, and where the memory
of his name is one of those associations which seem fa-
miliarly to haunt the banks of the historic river from
Thames Street to Westminster, apparently numbered not
more than 35,000 souls. But if, from the nature of the
case, no place was more exposed than London to the in-
roads of the Black Death, neither was any other so likely
elastically to recover from them. For the reign of Edward III. had witnessed a momentous advance in the prosperity of the capital—an advance reflecting itself in the
outward changes introduced during the same period into
the architecture of the city. Its wealth had grown larger
as its houses had grown higher; and mediæval London,
such as we are apt to picture it to ourselves, seems to have
derived those leading features which it so long retained, from
the days when Chaucer, with downcast but very observant
eyes, passed along its streets between Billingsgate and Aldgate. Still, here as elsewhere in England, the remembrance
of the most awful physical visitations which have ever be-
fallen the country must have long lingered; and, after all
has been said, it is wonderful that the traces of them
should be so exceedingly scanty in Chaucer's pages. Twice
only in his poems does he refer to the Plague: once in

an allegorical fiction which is of Italian if not of French origin, and where, therefore, no special reference to the ravages of the disease *in England* may be intended when Death is said to have " a thousand slain this pestilence"—

> " . . . He hath slain this year
> Hence over a mile, within a great villáge
> Both men and women, child and hind and page."

The other allusion is a more than half humorous one.   It occurs in the description of the *Doctor of Physic*, the grave graduate in purple surcoat and blue white-furred hood; nor, by the way, may this portrait itself be altogether without its use as throwing some light on the helplessness of fourteenth-century medical science. For though in all the world there was none like this doctor to *speak* of physic and of surgery; though he was a very perfect practitioner, and never at a loss for telling the cause of any malady and for supplying the patient with the appropriate drug, sent in by the doctor's old and faithful friends the apothecaries; though he was well versed in all the authorities from Æsculapius to the writer of the *Rosa Anglica* (who cures inflammation homœopathically by the use of red draperies); though, like a truly wise physician, he began at home by caring anxiously for his own digestion and for his peace of mind ("his study was but little in the Bible")—yet the basis of his scientific knowledge was "astronomy," *i. e.*, astrology, "the better part of medicine," as Roger Bacon calls it; together with that "natural magic" by which, as Chaucer elsewhere tells us, the famous among the learned have known how to make men whole or sick.   And there was one specific which, from a double point of view, Chaucer's Doctor of Physic esteemed very highly, and was loth to part with on frivo-

lous pretexts. He was but easy (*i. e.*, slack) of "dis-
pence":—

> "He keptë that he won in pestilence.
> For gold in physic is a cordial;
> Therefore he lovèd gold in speciál."

Meanwhile the ruling classes seem to have been left untouched in heart by these successive ill-met and ill-guard-
ed trials, which had first smitten the lower orders chiefly,
then the higher with the lower (if the Plague of 1349 had
swept off an archbishop, that of 1361 struck down, among
others, Henry, Duke of Lancaster, the father of Chaucer's
Duchess Blanche). Calamities such as these would assuredly have been treated as warnings sent from on high,
both in earlier times, when a Church better braced for the
due performance of its never-ending task, eagerly interpreted to awful ears the signs of the wrath of God, and
by a later generation, leavened in spirit by the self-search-
ing morality of Puritanism. But from the sorely-tried
third quarter of the fourteenth century the solitary voice
of Langland cries, as the voice of Conscience preaching
with her cross, that "these pestilences" are the penalty of
sin and of naught else. It is assuredly presumptuous for
one generation, without the fullest proof, to accuse another
of thoughtlessness or heartlessness; and though the classes
for which Chaucer mainly wrote, and with which he mainly
felt, were in all probability as little inclined to improve the
occasions of the Black Death as the middle classes of the
present day would be to fall on their knees after a season
of commercial ruin, yet signs are not wanting that in the
later years of the fourteenth century words of admonition
came to be not unfrequently spoken. The portents of the
eventful year 1382 called forth moralisings in English
verse, and the pestilence of 1391 a rhymed lamentation in

Latin; and at different dates in King Richard's reign, the poet Gower, Chaucer's contemporary and friend, inveighed both in Latin and in English, from his conservative point of view, against the corruption and sinfulness of society at large. But by this time the great peasant insurrection had added its warning, to which it was impossible to remain deaf.

A self-confident nation, however, is slow to betake itself to sackcloth and ashes. On the whole, it is clear that though the last years of Edward III. were a season of failure and disappointment—though from the period of the First Pestilence onwards the signs increase of the King's unpopularity and of the people's discontent—yet the over-burdened and enfeebled nation was brought almost as slowly as the King himself to renounce the proud position of a conquering power. In 1363 he had celebrated the completion of his fiftieth year; and three suppliant kings had at that time been gathered as satellites round the sun of his success. By 1371 he had lost all his allies, and nearly all the conquests gained by himself and the valiant Prince of Wales; and during the years remaining to him his subjects hated his rule and angrily assailed his favourites. From being a conquering power the English monarchy was fast sinking into an island which found it difficult to defend its own shores. There were times towards the close of Edward's, and early in his successor's reign, when matters would have gone hard with English traders, naturally desirous of having their money's worth for their subsidy of tonnage and poundage, and anxious, like their type the *Merchant* in Chaucer, that "the sea were kept for anything" between Middleburgh and Harwich, had not some of them, such as the Londoner, John Philpot, occasionally armed and manned a squadron of ships on their own ac-

count, in defiance of red tape and its censures. But in
the days when Chaucer and the generation with which he
grew up were young, the ardour of foreign conquest had
not yet died out in the land, and clergy and laity cheerful-
ly co-operated in bearing the burdens which military glory
has at all times brought with it for a civilised people. The
high spirit of the English nation, at a time when the decline in its fortunes was already near at hand (1366), is
evident from the answer given to the application from
Rome for the arrears of thirty-three years of the tribute
promised by King John, or rather from what must unmis-
takably have been the drift of that answer. Its terms are
unknown, but the demand was never afterwards repeated.

The power of England, in the period of an ascendency
to which she so tenaciously sought to cling, had not been
based only upon the valour of her arms. Our country
was already a rich one in comparison with most others in
Europe. Other purposes besides that of providing good
cheer for a robust generation were served by the wealth of
her great landed proprietors, and of the " worthy vava-
sours " (smaller land-owners) who, like Chaucer's *Franklin*
—a very Saint Julian or pattern of hospitality—knew not
what it was to be " without baked meat in the house,"
where their

> " Tables dormant in the hall alway
> Stood ready covered all the longë day."

From this source, and from the well-filled coffers of the
traders, came the laity's share of the expenses of those foreign wars which did so much to consolidate national feeling in England. The foreign companies of merchants
long contrived to retain the chief share of the banking
business and export trade assigned to them by the short-
sighted commercial policy of Edward III., and the weaving

and fishing industries of Hanseatic and Flemish immigrants had established an almost unbearable competition in our own ports and towns. But the active import trade, which already connected England with both nearer and remoter parts of Christendom, must have been largely in native hands; and English chivalry, diplomacy, and literature followed in the lines of the trade-routes to the Baltic and the Mediterranean. Our mariners, like their type the *Shipman* in Chaucer (an anticipation of the "Venturer" of later days, with the pirate as yet, perhaps, more strongly marked in him than the patriot),

> ". . . Knew well all the havens, as they were
> From Gothland, to the Cape of Finisterre,
> And every creek in Brittany and Spain."

Doubtless, as may be noticed in passing, much of the tendency on the part of our shipmen in this period to self-help, in offence as well as in defence, was due to the fact that the mercantile navy was frequently employed in expeditions of war, vessels and men being at times seized or impressed for the purpose by order of the Crown. On one of these occasions the port of Dartmouth, whence Chaucer at a venture ("for aught I wot") makes his *Shipman* hail, is found contributing a larger total of ships and men than any other port in England. For the rest, Flanders was certainly still far ahead of her future rival in wealth and in mercantile and industrial activity; as a manufacturing country she had no equal, and in trade the rival she chiefly feared was still the German Hansa. Chaucer's *Merchant* characteristically wears a "Flandrish beaver hat;" and it is no accident that the scene of the *Pardoner's Tale*, which begins with a description of "superfluity abominable," is laid in Flanders. In England,

indeed, the towns never came to domineer as they did in
the Netherlands. Yet, since no trading country will long
submit to be ruled by the landed interest only, so in proportion as the English towns, and London especially, grew
richer, their voices were listened to in the settlement of the
affairs of the nation. It might be very well for Chaucer
to close the description of his *Merchant* with what looks
very much like a fashionable writer's half sneer :—

> "Forsooth, he was a worthy man withal;
> But, truly, I wot not how men him call."

Yet not only was high political and social rank reached
by individual "merchant princes," such as the wealthy
William de la Pole, a descendant of whom is said (though
on unsatisfactory evidence) to have been Chaucer's grand-
daughter, but the government of the country came to be
very perceptibly influenced by the class from which they
sprang. On the accession of Richard II., two London citizens were appointed controllers of the war-subsidies
granted to the Crown; and in the Parliament of 1382 a
committee of fourteen merchants refused to entertain the
question of a merchants' loan to the King. The importance and self-consciousness of the smaller tradesmen and
handicraftsmen increased with that of the great merchants.
When, in 1393, King Richard II. marked the termination
of his quarrel with the City of London by a stately procession through "new Troy," he was welcomed, according
to the Friar who has commemorated the event in Latin
verse, by the trades in an array resembling an angelic
host; and among the crafts enumerated we recognise several of those represented in Chaucer's company of pilgrims
—by the *Carpenter*, the *Webbe* (Weaver), and the *Dyer*,
all clothed

> "... In one livery
> Of a solémn and great fraternity."

The middle class, in short, was learning to hold up its
head, collectively and individually.   The historical original
of Chaucer's *Host*—the actual Master Harry Bailly, vintner
and landlord of the Tabard Inn in Southwark, was likewise a member of Parliament, and very probably felt as
sure of himself in real life as the mimic personage bearing
his name does in its fictitious reproduction.   And he and
his fellows, the "poor and simple Commons"—for so
humble was the style they were wont to assume in their
addresses to the sovereign—began to look upon themselves, and to be looked upon, as a power in the State.
The London traders and handicraftsmen knew what it was
to be well-to-do citizens, and if they had failed to understand it, home monition would have helped to make it
clear to them :—

> "Well seemèd each of them a fair burgéss,
> For sitting in a guildhall on a dais.
> And each one for the wisdom that he can
> Was shapely for to be an alderman.
> They had enough of chattels and of rent,
> And very gladly would their wives assent;
> And, truly, else they had been much to blame.
> It is full fair to be yclept *madáme*,
> And fair to go to vigils all before,
> And have a mantle royally y-bore."

The English State had ceased to be the feudal monarchy—the ramification of contributory courts and camps
—of the crude days of William the Conqueror and his
successors.   The Norman lords and their English depend-
ents no longer formed two separate elements in the body-
politic.   In the great French wars of Edward III., the

English armies had no longer mainly consisted of the baronial levies. The nobles had indeed, as of old, ridden into battle at the head of their vassals and retainers; but the body of the force had been made up of Englishmen serving for pay, and armed with their national implement, the bow—such as Chaucer's *Yeoman* carried with him on the ride to Canterbury:—

> "A sheaf of peacock arrows bright and keen
> Under his belt he bare full thriftily.
> Well could he dress his tackle yeomanly:
> His arrows droopèd not with feathers low,
> And in his hand he bare a mighty bow."

The use of the bow was specially favoured by both Edward III. and his successor; and when, early in the next century, the chivalrous Scottish king, James I. (of whom mention will be made among Chaucer's poetic disciples) returned from his long English captivity to his native land, he had no more eager care than that his subjects should learn to emulate the English in the handling of their favourite weapon. Chaucer seems to be unable to picture an army without it, and we find him relating how, from ancient Troy,

> "Hector and many a worthy wight out went
> With spear in hand, and with their big bows bent."

No wonder that when the battles were fought by the people itself, and when the cost of the wars was to so large an extent defrayed by its self-imposed contributions, the Scottish and French campaigns should have called forth that national enthusiasm which found an echo in the songs of Lawrence Minot, as hearty war-poetry as has been composed in any age of our literature. They were put forth in 1352, and considering the unusual popularity they are said to have enjoyed, it is not impossible that they may have reached Chaucer's ears in his boyhood.

Before the final collapse of the great King's fortunes, and his death in a dishonoured old age, the ambition of his heir, the proudest hope of both dynasty and nation, had overleapt itself, and the Black Prince had preceded his father to the tomb. The good ship England (so sang a contemporary poet) was left without rudder or helm; and in a kingdom full of faction and discontent, the future of the Plantagenet throne depended on a child. While the young king's ambitious uncle, John of Gaunt, Duke of Lancaster (Chaucer's patron), was in nominal retirement, and his academical ally, Wyclif, was gaining popularity as the mouthpiece of the resistance to the papal demands, there were fermenting beneath the surface elements of popular agitation, which had been but little taken into account by the political factions of Edward the Third's reign, and by that part of its society with which Chaucer was more especially connected. But the multitude, whose turn, in truth, comes but rarely in the history of a nation, must every now and then make itself heard, although poets may seem all but blind and deaf to the tempest as it rises, and bursts, and passes away. Many causes had concurred to excite the insurrection which temporarily destroyed the influence of John of Gaunt, and which for long cast a deep shade upon the effects of the teaching of Wyclif. The acquisition of a measure of rights and power by the middle classes had caused a general swaying upwards; and throughout the peoples of Europe floated those dreams and speculations concerning the equality and fraternity of all men, which needed but a stimulus and an opportunity to assume the practical shape of a revolution. The melancholy thought which pervades Langland's *Vision* is still that of the helplessness of the poor; and the remedy to which he looks against the corruption of the governing classes is the advent of a superhuman king, whom he identifies with the ploughman himself, the representative of suffering humility.   But about the same time as that of the composition of this poem—or not long afterwards—Wyclif had sent forth among the people his " simple priests," who illustrated by contrast the conflict which his teaching exposed between the existing practice of the Church and the original documents of her faith.   The connexion between Wyclif's teaching and the peasants' insurrection under Richard II. is as undeniable as that between Luther's doctrines and the great social uprising in Germany a century and a half afterwards.   When, upon the declaration of the Papal Schism, Wyclif abandoned all hope of a reform of the Church from within, and, defying the injunctions of foe and friend alike, entered upon a course of theological opposition, the popular influence of his followers must have tended to spread a theory admitting of very easy application *ad hominem* — the theory, namely, that the tenure of all offices, whether spiritual or temporal, is justified only by the personal fitness of their occupants.   With such levelling doctrine, the Socialism of popular preachers like John Balle might seem to coincide with sufficient closeness; and since worthiness was not to be found in the holders of either spiritual or temporal authority, of either ecclesiastical or lay wealth, the time had palpably come for the poor man to enjoy his own again. Then, the advent of a weak government, over which a powerful kinsman of the King and unconcealed adversary of the Church was really seeking to recover the control, and the imposition of a tax coming home to all men except actual beggars, and filling serfdom's cup of bitterness to overflowing, supplied the opportunity, and the insurrection broke out. Its violence fell short of that of the French *Jacquerie* a quarter of a century earlier; but no doubt could exist as to its critical importance. As it happened, the revolt turned with special fury against the possessions of the Duke of Lancaster, whose sympathies with the cause of ecclesiastical reform it definitively extinguished.

After the suppression of this appalling movement by a party of Order, comprehending in it all who had anything to lose, a period of reaction ensued. In the reign of Richard II., whichever faction might be in the ascendant, and whatever direction the King's own sympathies may have originally taken, the last state of the peasantry was without doubt worse than the first. Wycliffism as an influence rapidly declined with the death of Wyclif himself, as it hardly could but decline, considering the absence from his teaching of any tangible system of Church government; and Lollardry came to be the popular name, or nickname, for any and every form of dissent from the existing system. Finally, Henry of Lancaster, John of Gaunt's son, mounted the throne as a sort of saviour of society—a favourite character for usurpers to pose in before the applauding assemblage of those who claim "a stake in the country." Chaucer's contemporary, Gower, whose wisdom was of the kind which goes with the times, who was in turn a flatterer of Richard and (by the simple expedient of a revised second edition of his *magnum opus*) a flatterer of Henry, offers better testimony than Chaucer to the conservatism of the upper classes of his age, and to the single-minded anxiety for the good times when

> "Justice of law is held;
> The privilege of royalty

2

> Is safe, and all the barony
> Worshippèd is in its estate.
> The people stands in obeisánce
> Under the rule of governánce."

Chaucer is less explicit, and may have been too little of a
politician by nature to care for preserving an outward con-
sistency in his incidental remarks concerning the lower
classes. In his *Clerk's Tale* he finds room for a very dubious commonplace about the " stormy people," its levity,
untruthfulness, indiscretion, fickleness, and garrulity, and
the folly of putting any trust in it. In his *Nun's Priest's
Tale* he further enlivens one of the liveliest descriptions
of a hue-and-cry ever put upon paper by a direct reference
to the Peasants' Rebellion :—

> " So hideous was the noise, ah *bencité !*
> That of a truth Jack Straw, and his meinie
> Not madë never shoutës half so shrill,
> When that they any Fleming meant to kill."

Assuredly, again, there is an unmistakeably conservative
tone in the *Ballad* purporting to have been sent by him
to King Richard, with its refrain as to all being " lost for
want of steadfastness," and its admonition to its sovereign
to

> " . . . Shew forth the sword of castigatión."

On the other hand, it would be unjust to leave unnoticed
the passage, at once powerful and touching, in the so-
called *Parson's Tale* (the sermon which closes the *Canterbury Tales* as Chaucer left them), in which certain lords
are reproached for taking of their bondmen *amercements*,
" which might more reasonably be called extortions than
amercements," while lords in general are commanded to be
good to their thralls (serfs), because " those that they clept

thralls, be God's people; for humble folks be Christ's friends; they be contubernially with the Lord." The solitary type, however, of the labouring man proper which Chaucer, in manifest remembrance of Langland's allegory, produces, is one which, beautiful and affecting as it is, has in it a flavour of the comfortable sentiment, that things are as they should be. This is—not, of course, the *Parson* himself, of which most significant character hereafter, but —the *Parson's* brother, the *Ploughman*. He is a true labourer and a good, religious and charitable. in his life, and always ready to pay his tithes. In short, he is a true Christian, but, at the same time, the ideal rather than the prototype, if one may so say, of the conservative working man.

Such were some, though of course some only, of the general currents of English public life in the latter half —Chaucer's half—of the fourteenth century. Its social features were naturally in accordance with the course of the national history. In the first place, the slow and painful process of amalgamation between the Normans and the English was still unfinished, though the reign of Edward III. went far towards completing what had rapidly advanced since the reigns of John and Henry III. By the middle of the fourteenth century English had become, or was just becoming, the common tongue of the whole nation. Among the political poems and songs preserved from the days of Edward III. and Richard II., not a single one composed on English soil is written in French. Parliament was opened by an English speech in the year 1363, and in the previous year the proceedings in the law courts were ordered to be conducted in the native tongue. Yet when Chaucer wrote his *Canterbury Tales*, it seems still to have continued the pedantic affectation of

a profession for its members, like Chaucer's *Man of Law*,
to introduce French law-terms into common conversation;
so that it is natural enough to find the *Summoner* following suit, and interlarding his *Tale* with the Latin scraps
picked up by him from the decrees and pleadings of the
ecclesiastical courts.   Meanwhile, manifold difficulties had
delayed or interfered with the fusion between the two
races, before the victory of the English language showed
this fusion to have been in substance accomplished.   One
of these difficulties, which has been sometimes regarded as
fundamental, has doubtless been exaggerated by national
feeling on either side; but that it existed is not to be denied.   Already in those ages the national character and
temperament of French and English differed largely from
one another; though the reasons why they so differed remain a matter of argument.   In a dialogue, dated from
the middle of the fourteenth century, the French inter-
locutor attributes this difference to the respective national
beverages: "*We* are nourished with the pure juice of the
grape, while naught but the dregs is sold to the English,
who will take anything for liquor that is liquid."   The
case is put with scarcely greater politeness by a living
French critic of high repute, according to whom the English, still weighted down by Teutonic phlegm, were drunken
gluttons, agitated at intervals by poetic enthusiasm, while
the Normans, on the other hand, lightened by their transplantation, and by the admixture of a variety of elements,
already found the claims of *esprit* developing themselves
within them.   This is an explanation which explains nothing—least of all, the problem: why the lively strangers
should have required the contact with insular phlegm in
order to receive the creative impulse—why, in other words,
Norman-French literature should have derived so enormous

an advantage from the transplantation of Normans to English ground. But the evil days when the literary labours of Englishmen had been little better than bond-service to the tastes of their foreign masters had passed away, since the Norman barons had, from whatever motive, invited the commons of England to take a share with them in the national councils. After this, the question of the relations between the two languages, and the wider one of the relations between the two nationalities, could only be decided by the peaceable adjustment of the influences exercised by the one side upon the other. The Norman noble, his ideas, and the expression they found in forms of life and literature, had henceforth, so to speak, to stand on their merits; the days of their dominion, as a matter of course, had passed away.

Together with not a little of their political power, the Norman nobles of Chaucer's time had lost something of the traditions of their order. Chivalry had not quite come to an end with the Crusades; but it was a difficult task to maintain all its laws, written and unwritten, in these degenerate days. No laurels were any longer to be gained in the Holy Land; and though the campaigns of the great German Order against the pagans of Prussia and Lithuania attracted the service of many an English knight—in the middle of the century, Henry, Duke of Lancaster, fought there, as his grandson, afterwards King Henry IV., did forty years later—yet the substitute was hardly adequate in kind. Of the great mediæval companies of Knights, the most famous had, early in the century, perished under charges which were undoubtedly in the main foul fictions, but at the same time were only too much in accord with facts betokening an unmistakeable decay of the true spirit of chivalry; before the century closed, lawyers were rolling

parchments in the halls of the Templars by the Thames.
Thus, though the age of chivalry had not yet ended, its
supremacy was already on the wane, and its ideal was
growing dim.   In the history of English chivalry the
reign of Edward III. is memorable, not only for the foundation of our most illustrious order of knighthood, but
likewise for many typical acts of knightly valour and cour-
tesy, as well on the part of the King when in his better
days, as on that of his heroic son.   Yet it cannot be by
accident that an undefinable air of the old-fashioned clings
to that most delightful of all Chaucer's character sketches,
the *Knight* of the *Canterbury Tales.*   His warlike deeds
at Alexandria, in Prussia, and elsewhere, may be illustrated
from those of more than one actual knight of the times;
and the whole description of him seems founded on one
by a French poet of King John of Bohemia, who had at
least the external features of a knight of the old school.
The chivalry, however, which was in fashion as the century
advanced, was one outwardly far removed from the sturdy
simplicity of Chaucer's *Knight,* and inwardly often rotten
in more than one vital part.   In show and splendour a
higher point was probably reached in Edward III.'s than
in any preceding reign.   The extravagance in dress which
prevailed in this period is too well known a characteristic
of it to need dwelling upon.   Sumptuary laws in vain
sought to restrain this foible; and it rose to such a pitch
as even to oblige men, lest they should be precluded from
indulging in gorgeous raiment, to abandon hospitality, a
far more amiable species of excess.   When the kinds of
clothing respectively worn by the different classes served
as distinctions of rank, the display of splendour in one
class could hardly fail to provoke emulation in the others.
The long-lived English love for "crying" colours shows

itself amusingly enough in the early pictorial representa-
tions of several of Chaucer's Canterbury pilgrims, though
in floridity of apparel, as of speech, the youthful *Squire*
bears away the bell :—

> "Embroidered was he, as it were a mead
> All full of freshest flowers, white and red."

But of the artificiality and extravagance of the costumes
of these times we have direct contemporary evidence, and
loud contemporary complaints. Now, it is the jagged cut
of the garments, punched and shredded by the man-milli-
ner ; now, the wide and high collars and the long-pointed
boots, which attract the indignation of the moralist ; at
one time he inveighs against the "horrible disordinate
scantness" of the clothing worn by gallants, at another
against the "outrageous array" in which ladies love to ex-
hibit their charms. The knights' horses are decked out
with not less finery than are the knights themselves, with
"curious harness, as in saddles and bridles, cruppers and
breastplates, covered with precious clothing, and with bars
and plates of gold and silver." And though it is hazardous to stigmatize the fashions of any one period as specially grotesque, yet it is significant of this age to find the
reigning court beauty appearing at a tournament robed as
Queen of the Sun ; while even a lady from a manufacturing district, the *Wife of Bath*, makes the most of her opportunities to be seen as well as to see. Her "kerchiefs"
were "full fine" of texture, and weighed, one might be
sworn, ten pound—

> "That on a Sunday were upon her head,
> Her hosen too were of fine scarlet red,
> Full straight y-tied, and shoes full moist and new.
>
> *   *   *   *   *   *

> Upon an ambler easily she sat,
> Y-wimpled well, and on her head a hat,
> As broad as is a buckler or a targe."

So, with a foot-mantle round her hips, and a pair of sharp spurs on her feet, she looked as defiant as any self-conscious Amazon of any period. It might, perhaps, be shown how, in more important artistic efforts than fashions of dress, this age displayed its aversion from simplicity and moderation. At all events, the love of the florid and overloaded declares itself in what we know concerning the social life of the nobility, as, for instance, we find that life reflected in the pages of Froissart, whose counts and lords seem neither to clothe themselves nor to feed themselves, nor to talk, pray, or swear like ordinary mortals. The *Vows of the Heron*, a poem of the earlier part of King Edward III.'s reign, contains a choice collection of strenuous knightly oaths; and in a humbler way the rest of the population very naturally imitated the parlance of their rulers, and in the words of the *Parson's Tale*, "dismembered Christ by soul, heart, bones, and body."

But there is one very much more important feature to be noticed in the social life of the nobility, for whom Chaucer's poetry must have largely replaced the French verse in which they had formerly delighted. The relation between knight and lady plays a great part in the history as well as in the literature of the later Plantagenet period; and incontestably its conceptions of this relation still retained much of the pure sentiment belonging to the best and most fervent times of Christian chivalry. The highest religious expression which has ever been given to man's sense of woman's mission, as his life's comfort and crown, was still a universally dominant belief. To the Blessed Virgin, King Edward III. dedicated his principal religious foundation; and Chaucer, to whatever extent his opinions or sentiments may have been in accordance with ideas of ecclesiastical reform, displays a pious devotion towards the foremost Saint of the Church. The lyric entitled the *Praise of Women*, in which she is enthusiastically recognized as the representative of the whole of her sex, is generally rejected as not Chaucer's; but the elaborate "Orison to the Holy Virgin," beginning

"Mother of God, and Virgin undefiled,"

seems to be correctly described as *Oratio Gallfridi Chaucer;* and in *Chaucer's A. B. C., called La Prière de Notre Dame*, a translation by him from a French original, we have a long address to the Blessed Virgin in twenty-three stanzas, each of which begins with one of the letters of the alphabet arranged in proper succession. Nor, apart from this religious sentiment, had men yet altogether lost sight of the ideal of true knightly love, destined though this ideal was to be obscured in the course of time, until at last the *Mort d'Arthure* was the favourite literary nourishment of the minions and mistresses of Edward IV.'s degenerate days. In his *Book of the Duchess* Chaucer has left us a picture of true knightly love, together with one of true maiden purity. The lady celebrated in this poem was loth, merely for the sake of coquetting with their exploits, to send her knights upon errands of chivalry—

". . . Into Walachy,
To Prussia, and to Tartary,
To Alexandria or Turkéy."

And doubtless there was many a gentle knight or squire to whom might have been applied the description given by the heroine of Chaucer's *Troilus and Cressid* of her lover, and of that which attracted her in him:—

2*

"For trust ye well that your estate royál,
 Nor vain delight, nor only worthiness
 Of you in war or tourney martial,
 Nor pomp, array, nobility, richés,
 Of these none made me rue on your distress;
 But moral virtue, grounded upon truth,
 That was the cause I first had on you ruth.

"And gentle heart, and manhood that ye had,
 And that ye had (as méthought) in despite
 Everything that tended unto bad,
 As rudeness, and as popular appetite,
 And that your reason bridled your delight;
 'Twas these did make 'bove every creatúre
 That I was yours, and shall while I may 'dure."

And if true affection under the law still secured the sympathy of the better-balanced part of society, so the vice of
those who made war upon female virtue, or the insolence
of those who falsely boasted of their conquests, still incurred its resentment.   Among the companies which in the
House o Fame sought the favour of its mistress, Chaucer
vigorously satirises the would-be lady-killers, who were content with the *reputation* of accomplished seducers; and in
Troilus and Cressid a shrewd observer exclaims with the
utmost vivacity against

"Such sort of folk—what shall I clepe them? what?
 That vaunt themselves of women, and by name,
 That yet to them ne'er promised this or that,
 Nor knew them more, in sooth, than mine old hat."

The same easy but sagacious philosopher (Pandarus) observes that the harm which is in this world springs as often from folly as from malice.   But a deeper feeling ani-
mates the lament of the "good Alceste," in the Prologue

to the *Legend of Good Women*, that among men the betrayal of women is now "held a game." So indisputably it was already often esteemed, in too close an accordance with examples set in the highest places in the land.
If we are to credit an old tradition, a poem in which Chaucer narrates the amours of Mars and Venus was written
by him at the request of John of Gaunt, to celebrate the
adultery of the duke's sister-in-law with a nobleman, to
whom the injured kinsman afterwards married one of his
own daughters! But nowhere was the deterioration of
sentiment on this head more strongly typified than in Edward III. himself. The King, who (if the pleasing tale
be true which gave rise to some beautiful scenes in an old
English drama) had in his early days royally renounced an
unlawful passion for the fair Countess of Salisbury, came
to be accused of at once violating his conjugal duty and
neglecting his military glory for the sake of strange wom-
en's charms. The founder of the Order of the Garter—
the device of which enjoined purity even of thought as a
principle of conduct — died in the hands of a rapacious
courtesan. Thus, in England, as in France, the ascendency
is gained by ignobler views concerning the relation between the sexes—a relation to which the whole system of
chivalry owed a great part of its vitality, and on the view
of which prevailing in the most influential class of any
nation, the social health of that nation must inevitably in
no small measure depend. Meanwhile, the artificialities by
means of which in France, up to the beginning of the fifteenth century, it was sought to keep alive an organised
system of sentimentality in the social dealings between
gentlemen and ladies, likewise found admission in England,
but only in a modified degree. Here the fashion in question asserted itself only, or chiefly, in our poetic literature,

and in the adoption by it of such fancies as the praise and
worship of the daisy, with which we meet in the Prologue
to Chaucer's *Legend of Good Women*, and in the *Flower
and the Leaf*, a most pleasing poem (suggested by a French
model), which it is unfortunately no longer possible to number among his genuine works. The poem of the *Court
of Love*, which was likewise long erroneously attributed
to him, may be the original work of an English author;
but in any case its main contents are a mere adaptation of
a peculiar outgrowth on a foreign soil of conceptions common to chivalry in general.

Of another force, which in the Middle Ages shared with
chivalry (though not with it alone) the empire over the
minds of men, it would certainly be rash to assert that its
day was passing away in the latter half of the fourteenth
century. It has, indeed, been pointed out that the date at
which Wyclif's career as a reformer may be said to have
begun almost coincides with that of the climax and first
decline of feudal chivalry in England. But, without seeking to interpret coincidences, we know that, though the
influence of the Christian Church, and that of its Roman
branch in particular, has asserted and re-asserted itself in
various ways and degrees in various ages, yet in England,
as elsewhere, the epoch of its moral omnipotence had come
to an end many generations before the disruption of its
external framework. In the fourteenth century men had
long ceased to look for the mediation of the Church between an overbearing Crown and a baronage and common-
alty eager for the maintenance of their rights or for the
assertion of their claims. On the other hand, the conflicts
which still recurred between the temporal power and the
Church had as little reference as ever to spiritual concerns.
Undoubtedly, the authority of the Church over the minds

of the people still depended in the main upon the spiritual influence she exercised over them; and the desire for a reformation of the Church, which was already making itself felt in a gradually widening sphere, was, by the great majority of those who cherished it, held perfectly compatible with a recognition of her authority. The world, it has been well said, needed an enquiry extending over three centuries, in order to learn to walk without the aid of the Church of Rome. Wyclif, who sought to emancipate the human conscience from reliance upon any earthly authority intermediate between the soul and its Maker, reckoned without his generation; and few, except those with whom audacity took the place of argument, followed him to the extreme results of his speculations. The Great Schism rather stayed than promoted the growth of an English feeling against Rome, since it was now no longer necessary to acknowledge a Pope who seemed the henchman of the arch-foe across the narrow seas.

But although the progress of English sentiment towards the desire for liberation from Rome was to be interrupted by a long and seemingly decisive reaction, yet in the fourteenth, as in the sixteenth, century the most active cause of the alienation of the people from the Church was the conduct of the representatives of the Church themselves. The Reformation has most appropriately retained in history a name at first unsuspiciously applied to the removal of abuses in the ecclesiastical administration and in the life of the clergy. What aid could be derived by those who really hungered for spiritual food, or what strength could accrue to the thoughtless faith of the light-hearted majority, from many of the most common varieties of the English ecclesiastic of the later Middle Ages? Apart from the Italian and other foreign holders of English benefices,

who left their flocks to be tended by deputy, and to be
shorn by an army of the most offensive kind of tax-gath-
erers, the native clergy included many species, but among
them few which, to the popular eye, seemed to embody a
high ideal of religious life. The times had by no means
come to an end when many of the higher clergy sought
to vie with the lay lords in warlike prowess. Perhaps
the martial Bishop of Norwich, who, after persecuting the
heretics at home, had commanded an army of crusaders in
Flanders, levied on behalf of Pope Urban VI. against the
anti-Pope Clement VII. and his adherents, was in the poet
Gower's mind when he complains that while

> ". . . The law is rulèd so,
> That clerks unto the war intend,
> I wot not how they should amend
> The woeful world in other things,
> And so make peace between the kings
> After the law of charity,
> Which is the duty properly
> Belonging unto the priesthóod."

A more general complaint, however, was that directing
itself against the extravagance and luxury of life in which
the dignified clergy indulged. The cost of these unspir-
itual pleasures the great prelates had ample means for de-
fraying in the revenues of their sees; while lesser digni-
taries had to be active in levying their dues or the fines
of their courts, lest everything should flow into the recep-
tacles of their superiors. So in Chaucer's *Friar's Tale* an
unfriendly Regular says of an archdeacon :—

> " For smallë tithes and for small offering
> He made the people piteously to sing.
> For ere the bishop caught them on his hook,
> They were down in the archëdeacon's book."

As a matter of course, the worthy who filled the office of *Summoner* to the court of the archdeacon in question had a keen eye for the profitable improprieties subject to its penalties, and was aided in his efforts by the professional abettors of vice whom he kept "ready to his hand." Nor is it strange that the undisguised worldliness of many members of the clerical profession should have reproduced itself in other lay subordinates, even in the parish clerks, at all times apt to copy their betters, though we would fain hope such was not the case with the parish clerk, "the jolly Absalom" of the *Miller's Tale*. The love of gold had corrupted the acknowledged chief guardians of incorruptible treasures, even though few may have avowed this love as openly as the "idle" *Canon*, whose *Yeoman* had so strange a tale to tell to the Canterbury pilgrims concerning his master's absorbing devotion to the problem of the multiplication of gold. To what a point the popular discontent with the vices of the higher secular clergy had advanced in the last decennium of the century, may be seen from the poem called the *Complaint of the Plough-man*—a production pretending to be by the same hand which in the *Vision* had dwelt on the sufferings of the people and on the sinfulness of the ruling classes. Justly or unjustly, the indictment was brought against the priests of being the agents of every evil influence among the people, the soldiers of an army of which the true head was not God, but Belial.

In earlier days the Church had known how to compensate the people for the secular clergy's neglect, or imperfect performance, of its duties. But in no respect had the ecclesiastical world more changed than in this. The older monastic Orders had long since lost themselves in unconcealed worldliness; how, for instance, had the Bene-

dictines changed their character since the remote times
when their Order had been the principal agent in revivify-
ing the religion of the land! Now, they were taunted
with their very name, as having been bestowed upon them
"by antiphrasis," *i. e.*, by contraries. From many of their
monasteries, and from the inmates who dwelt in these
comfortable halls, had vanished even all pretence of disguise. Chaucer's *Monk* paid no attention to the rule of
St. Benedict, and of his disciple St. Maur,

> "Because that it was old and somewhat strait;"

and preferred to fall in with the notions of later times.
He was an "outrider, that loved venery," and whom his
tastes and capabilities would have well qualified for the
dignified post of abbot. He had "full many a dainty
horse" in his stable, and the swiftest of greyhounds to
boot; and rode forth gaily, clad in superfine furs and a
hood elegantly fastened with a gold pin, and tied into a
love-knot at the "greater end," while the bridle of his steed
jingled as if its rider had been as good a knight as any of
them—this last, by the way, a mark of ostentation against
which Wyclif takes occasion specially to inveigh. This
Monk (and Chaucer must say that he was wise in his generation) could not understand why he should study books
and unhinge his mind by the effort; life was not worth
having at the price; and no one knew better to what use
to put the pleasing gift of existence. Hence mine host
of the Tabard, a very competent critic, had reason for the
opinion which he communicated to the Monk:—

> "It is a noble pasture where thou go'st;
> Thou art not like a penitent or ghost."

In the Orders of nuns, certain corresponding features were

becoming usual. But little in the way of religious guid-
ance could fall to the lot of a sisterhood presided over by
such a *Prioress* as Chaucer's Madame Eglantine, whose
mind—possibly because her nunnery fulfilled the functions
of a finishing school for young ladies—was mainly devoted to French and deportment, or by such a one as the
historical Lady Juliana Berners, of a rather later date,
whose leisure hours produced treatises on hunting and
hawking, and who would probably have, on behalf of her
own sex, echoed the *Monk's* contempt for the prejudice
against the participation of the Religious in field-sports:—

> "He gave not for that text a pullèd hen
> That saith, that hunters be no holy men."

On the other hand, neither did the Mendicant Orders, in-
stituted at a later date purposely to supply what the older
Orders, as well as the secular clergy, seemed to have grown
incapable of furnishing, any longer satisfy the reason of
their being. In the fourteenth century the Dominicans, or
Black Friars, who at London dwelt in such magnificence
that king and Parliament often preferred a sojourn with
them to abiding at Westminster, had in general grown accustomed to concentrate their activity upon the spiritual
direction of the higher classes. But though they counted
among them Englishmen of eminence (one of these was
Chaucer's friend, "the philosophical Strode"), they, in
truth, never played a more than secondary part in this
country, to whose soil the delicate machinery of the Inquisition, of which they were by choice the managers, was
never congenial. Of far greater importance for the population of England at large was the Order of the Franciscans, or (as they were here wont to call themselves or to
be called) Minorites or Grey Friars. To them the poor

had habitually looked for domestic ministrations, and for
the inspiring and consoling eloquence of the pulpit; and
they had carried their labours into the midst of the suffering population, not afraid of association with that poverty which they were by their vow themselves bound to espouse, or of contact with the horrors of leprosy and the
plague.　Departing from the short-sighted policy of their
illustrious founder, they had become a learned as well as
a ministering and preaching Order; and it was precisely
from among them that, at Oxford and elsewhere, sprang a
succession of learned monks, whose names are inseparably
connected with some of the earliest English growths of
philosophical speculation and scientific research.　Nor is
it possible to doubt that in the middle of the thirteenth
century the monks of this Order at Oxford had exercised
an appreciable influence upon the beginnings of a political
struggle of unequalled importance for the progress of our
constitutional life.　But in the Franciscans also the fourteenth century witnessed a change, which may be described as a gradual loss of the qualities for which they
had been honourably distinguished; and in England, as
elsewhere, the spirit of the words which Dante puts into
the mouth of St. Francis of Assisi was being verified by
his degenerate children :—

> "So soft is flesh of mortals, that on earth
> A good beginning doth no longer last
> Than while an oak may bring its fruit to birth."

Outwardly, indeed, the Grey Friars might still often seem
what their predecessors had been, and might thus retain
a powerful influence over the unthinking crowd, and to
sheer worldlings appear, as heretofore, to represent a trou-
blesome *memento* of unexciting religious obligations;
"Preach not," says Chaucer's *Host*,

"... As friars do in Lent,
That they for our old sins may make us weep,
Nor in such wise thy tale make us to sleep."

But in general men were beginning to suspect the motives
as well as to deride the practices of the Friars, to accuse
them of lying against St. Francis, and to desiderate for
them an actual abode of fire, resembling that of which, in
their favourite religious shows, they were wont to present
the mimic semblance to the multitude. It was they who
became in England, as elsewhere, the purveyors of charms
and the organisers of pious frauds, while the learning for
which their Order had been famous was withering away
into the yellow leaf of scholasticism. The Friar in general
became the common butt of literary satire; and though
the populace still remained true to its favourite guides, a
reaction was taking place in favour of the secular as against
the regular clergy in the sympathies of the higher classes,
and in the spheres of society most open to intellectual influences. The monks and the London multitude were at
one time united against John of Gaunt, but it was from
the ranks of the secular clergy that Wyclif came forth to
challenge the ascendency of Franciscan scholasticism in
his university. Meanwhile the poet who in the *Poor Parson of the Town* paints his ideal of a Christian minister—
simple, poor, and devoted to his holy work—has nothing
but contempt for the friars at large, and for the whole machinery worked by them, half effete, and half spasmodic,
and altogether sham. In King Arthur's time, says that
accurate and unprejudiced observer, the *Wife of Bath*, the
land was filled with fairies—*now* it is filled with friars as
thick as motes in the beam of the sun. Among them
there is the *Pardoner*—*i. e.*, seller of pardons (indulgences)
—with his "haughty" sermons, delivered "by rote" to

congregation after congregation in the self-same words, and everywhere accompanied by the self-same tricks of anecdotes and jokes—with his Papal credentials, and with the pardons he has brought from Rome "all hot"—and with precious relics to rejoice the hearts of the faithful, and to fill his own pockets with the proceeds: to wit, a pillowcase covered with the veil of Our Lady, and a piece of the sail of the ship in which St. Peter went out fishing on the Lake of Gennesareth. This worthy, who lays bare his own motives with unparalleled cynical brutality, is manifestly drawn from the life; or the portrait could not have been accepted which was presented alike by Chaucer, and by his contemporary Langland, and (a century and a half later) in the plagiarism of the orthodox Catholic John Heywood. There, again, is the *Limitour*, a friar licensed to beg, and to hear confession and grant absolution, within the *limits* of a certain district. He is described by Chaucer with so much humour that one can hardly suspect much exaggeration in the sketch. In him we have the truly popular ecclesiastic who springs from the people, lives among the people, and feels with the people. He is the true friend of the poor, and being such, has, as one might say, his finger in every pie; for "a fly and a friar will fall in every dish and every business." His readily-proffered arbitration settles the differences of the humbler classes at the "love-days," a favourite popular practice noted already in the *Vision* of Langland; nor is he a niggard of the mercies which he is privileged to dispense :—

> "Full sweetly did he hear confessión,
> And pleasant was his absolutión.
> He was an easy man to give penánce,
> Whereso wist to have a good pittánce;

> For unto a poor Order for to give,
> Is signë that a man is well y-shrive;
> For if he gave, he durstë make a vaunt
> He wistë that a man was répentant.
> For many a man so hard is of his heart
> He can not weep although he sorely smart.
> Therefore, instead of weeping and of prayers,
> Men must give silver to the poorë Freres."

Already in the French *Roman de la Rose* the rivalry between the Friars and the Parish Priests is the theme of
much satire, evidently unfavourable to the former and favourable to the latter; but in England, where Langland
likewise dwells upon the jealousy between them, it was
specially accentuated by the assaults of Wyclif upon the
Mendicant Orders.   Wyclif's Simple Priests, who at first
ministered with the approval of the Bishops, differed from
the Mendicants—first, by not being beggars; and, second-
ly, by being poor.   They might, perhaps, have themselves
ultimately played the part of a new Order in England,
had not Wyclif himself, by rejecting the cardinal dogma
of the Church, severed these followers of his from its or-
ganism and brought about their suppression.   The question as to Chaucer's own attitude towards the Wycliffite
movement will be more conveniently touched upon below;
but the tone is unmistakable of the references or allusions
to Lollardry which he occasionally introduces into the
mouth of his *Host*, whose voice is that *vox populi* which
the upper and middle classes so often arrogate to themselves.   Whatever those classes might desire, it was not
to have "cockle sown" by unauthorised intruders "in the
corn" of their ordinary instruction.   Thus there is a tone
of genuine attachment to the "vested interest" principle,
and of aversion from all such interlopers as lay preachers

and the like, in the *Host's* exclamation, uttered after the
Reeve has been (in his own style) "sermoning" on the
topic of old age :—

> "What availeth all this wit ?
> What ? should we speak all day of Holy Writ ?
> The devil surely made a reeve to preach ;"

for which he is as well suited as a cobbler would be for
turning mariner or physician !

Thus, then, in the England of Chaucer's days we find
the Church still in possession of vast temporal wealth and
of great power and privileges—as well as of means for en-
forcing unity of profession which the legislation of the
Lancastrian dynasty, stimulated by the prevailing fears of
heresy, was still further to increase.   On the other hand,
we find the influence of the clergy over the minds of the
people diminished, though not extinguished.   This was, in
the case of the higher secular clergy, partly attributable to
their self-indulgence or neglect of their functions, partly
to their having been largely superseded by the Regulars
in the control of the religious life of the people.   The
Orders we find no longer at the height of their influence,
but still powerful by their wealth, their numbers, their
traditional hold upon the lower classes, and their deter-
mination to retain this hold even by habitually resorting
to the most dubious of methods.   Lastly, we find in the
lower secular clergy, and doubtless may also assume it to
have lingered among some of the regular, some of the salt
left whose savour consists in a single-minded and humble
resolution to maintain the highest standard of a religious
life.   But such "clerks" as these are at no times the most
easily found, because it is not they who are always running
"unto London, unto St. Paul's," on urgent private affairs.

What wonder that the real teaching of Wyclif, of which
the full significance could hardly be understood but by a
select few, should have virtually fallen dead upon his generation, to which the various agitations and agitators, often
mingling ideas of religious reform with social and political
grievances, seemed to be identical in character and alike
to require suppression! In truth, of course, these movements and their agents were often very different from one
another in their ends, and were not to be suppressed by
the same processes.

It should not be forgotten that in this century learning
was, though only very gradually, ceasing to be a possession
of the clergy alone. Much doubt remains as to the extent
of education—if a little reading and less writing deserve
the name—among the higher classes in this period of our
national life. A cheering sign appears in the circumstance
that the legal deeds of this age begin to bear signatures,
and a reference to John of Trevisa would bear out Hallam's
conjecture, that in the year 1400 "the average instruction
of an English gentleman of the first class would compre-
hend common reading and writing, a considerable knowledge of French, and a slight tincture of Latin." Certain
it is that in this century the barren teaching of the Universities advanced but little towards the true end of all
academical teaching—the encouragement and spread of
the highest forms of national culture. To what use could
a gentleman of Edward III.'s or Richard II.'s day have
put the acquirements of a *Clerk of Oxenford* in Aristoteli-
an logic, supplemented perhaps by a knowledge of Priscian,
and the rhetorical works of Cicero? Chaucer's scholar,
however much his learned modesty of manner and sententious brevity of speech may commend him to our sympathy and taste, is a man wholly out of the world in which

he lives, though a dependent on its charity even for the
means with which to purchase more of his beloved books.
Probably no trustworthier conclusions as to the literary
learning and studies of those days are to be derived from
any other source than from a comparison of the few cata-
logues of contemporary libraries remaining to us; and
these help to show that the century was approaching its
close before a few sparse rays of the first dawn of the
Italian Renascence reached England. But this ray was
communicated neither through the clergy nor through the
Universities; and such influence as was exercised by it
upon the national mind was directly due to profane poets
—men of the world, who, like Chaucer, quoted authorities
even more abundantly than they used them, and made
some of their happiest discoveries after the fashion in
which the *Oxford Clerk* came across Petrarch's Latin version of the story of Patient Grissel: as it were by accident.   There is only too ample a justification for leaving
aside the records of the history of learning in England
during the latter half of the fourteenth century in any
sketch of the main influences which in that period determined or affected the national progress. It was not by
his theological learning that Wyclif was brought into living contact with the current of popular thought and feeling.   The Universities were thriving exceedingly on the
scholastic glories of previous ages; but the ascendency
was passing away to which Oxford had attained over Paris
—during the earlier middle ages, and again in the fifteenth
century until the advent of the Renascence, the central
university of Europe in the favourite study of scholastic
philosophy and theology.

But we must turn from particular classes and ranks of
men to the whole body of the population, exclusively of

that great section of it which unhappily lay outside the observation of any but a very few writers, whether poets or historians. In the people at large we may, indeed, easily discern in this period the signs of an advance towards that self-government which is the true foundation of our national greatness. But, on the other hand, it is impossible not to observe how, while the moral ideas of the people were still under the control of the Church, the State in its turn still ubiquitously interfered in the settlement of the conditions of social existence, fixing prices, controlling personal expenditure, regulating wages. Not until England had fully attained to the character of a commercial country, which it was coming gradually to assume, did its inhabitants begin to understand the value of that which has gradually come to distinguish ours among the nations of Europe, viz., the right of individual Englishmen, as well as of the English people, to manage their own affairs for themselves. This may help to explain what can hardly fail to strike a reader of Chaucer and of the few contemporary remains of our literature. About our national life in this period, both in its virtues and in its vices, there is something—it matters little whether we call it— childlike or childish; in its " apert " if not in its " privy " sides it lacks the seriousness belonging to men and to generations, who have learnt to control themselves, instead of relying on the control of others.

In illustration of this assertion, appeal might be made to several of the most salient features in the social life of the period. The extravagant expenditure in dress, fostered by a love of pageantry of various kinds encouraged by both chivalry and the Church, has been already referred to ; it was by no means distinctive of any one class of the population. Among the friars who went about preaching

3

homilies on the people's favourite vices some humorous
rogues may, like the *Pardoner* of the *Canterbury Tales*,
have made a point of treating their own favourite vice as
their one and unchangeable text :—

> " My theme is always one, and ever was :
>   *Radix malorum est cupiditas.*"

But others preferred to dwell on specifically lay sins;
and these moralists occasionally attributed to the love of
expenditure on dress the impoverishment of the kingdom,
forgetting, in their ignorance of political economy and defiance of common sense, that this result was really due to
the endless foreign wars.   Yet, in contrast with the pomp
and ceremony of life, upon which so great an amount of
money and time and thought was wasted, are noticeable
shortcomings by no means uncommon in the case of un-
developed civilisations (as, for instance, among the most
typically childish or childlike nationalities of the Europe
of our own day), viz., discomfort and uncleanliness of all
sorts.   To this may be added the excessive fondness for
sports and pastimes of all kinds, in which nations are apt-
est to indulge before or after the era of their highest efforts—the desire to make life one long holiday, dividing
it between tournaments and the dalliance of courts of
love, or between archery-meetings (skilfully substituted by
royal command for less useful exercises), and the seduc-
tive company of " tumblers," " fruiterers," and " waferers."
Furthermore, one may notice in all classes a far from erad-
icated inclination to superstitions of every kind—whether
those encouraged or those discouraged[1] by the Church—

---

[1] " For holy Church's faith, in our belief,
    Suffereth no illusion us to grieve."
                                    The Franklin's Tale.

an inclination unfortunately fostered rather than checked by the uncertain gropings of contemporary science. Hence, the credulous acceptance of relics like those sold by the *Pardoner*, and of legends like those related to Chaucer's Pilgrims by the *Prioress* (one of the numerous repetitions of a cruel calumny against the Jews), and by the *Second Nun* (the supra-sensual story of Saint Cecilia). Hence, on the other hand, the greedy hunger for the marvels of astrology and alchemy, notwithstanding the growing scepticism even of members of a class represented by Chaucer's *Franklin* towards

> "... Such folly
> As in our days is not held worth a fly,"

and notwithstanding the exposure of fraud by repentant or sickened accomplices, such as the gold-making *Canon's Yeoman*. Hence, again, the vitality of such quasi-scientific fancies as the magic mirror, of which miraculous instrument the *Squire's* "half-told story" describes a specimen, referring to the incontestable authority of Aristotle and others, who write "in their lives" concerning quaint mirrors and perspective glasses, as is well known to those who have "heard the books" of these sages. Hence, finally, the corresponding tendency to eschew the consideration of serious religious questions, and to leave them to clerks, as if they were crabbed problems of theology. For, in truth, while the most fertile and fertilising ideas of the Middle Ages had exhausted, or were rapidly coming to exhaust, their influence upon the people, the forms of the doctrines of the Church—even of the most stimulative as well as of the most solemn among them—had grown hard and stiff. To those who received, if not to those who taught, these doctrines they seemed alike lifeless, unless translated into the terms of the merest earthly transactions or the language of purely human relations. And thus, paradoxical as it might seem, cool-headed and conscientious rulers of the Church thought themselves on occasion called upon to restrain rather than to stimulate the religious ardour of the multitude—fed as the flame was by very various materials. Perhaps no more characteristic narrative has come down to us from the age of the poet of the *Canterbury Tales* than the story of Bishop (afterwards Archbishop) Sudbury and the Canterbury Pilgrims. In the year 1370 the land was agitated through its length and breadth, on the occasion of the fourth jubilee of the national saint, Thomas the Martyr. The pilgrims were streaming in numbers along the familiar Kentish road, when, on the very vigil of the feast, one of their companies was accidentally met by the Bishop of London. They demanded his blessing; but, to their astonishment and indignation, he seized the occasion to read a lesson to the crowd on the uselessness to unrepentant sinners of the plenary indulgences, for the sake of which they were wending their way to the Martyr's shrine. The rage of the multitude found a mouthpiece in a soldier, who loudly upbraided the Bishop for stirring up the people against St. Thomas, and warned him that a shameful death would befall him in consequence. The multitude shouted *Amen* —and one is left to wonder whether any of the pious pilgrims who resented Bishop Sudbury's manly truthfulness swelled the mob which eleven years later butchered "the plunderer," as it called him, "of the Commons." It is such glimpses as this which show us how important the Church had become towards the people. Worse was to ensue before the better came; in the mean time, the nation was in that stage of its existence when the innocence of the child was fast losing itself, without the self-control of the man having yet taken its place.

But the heart of England was sound the while. The national spirit of enterprise was not dead in any class, from knight to shipman; and faithfulness and chastity in woman were still esteemed the highest though not the universal virtues of her sex. The value of such evidence as the mind of a great poet speaking in his works furnishes for a knowledge of the times to which he belongs is inestimable; for it shows us what has survived, as well as what was doomed to decay, in the life of the nation with which that mind was in sensitive sympathy. And it therefore seemed not inappropriate to approach, in the first instance, from this point of view, the subject of this biographical essay — Chaucer, "the poet of the dawn:" for in him there are many things significant of the age of transition in which he lived; in him the mixture of Frenchman and Englishman is still in a sense incomplete, as that of their language is in the diction of his poems. His gaiety of heart is hardly English; nor is his willing (though, to be sure, not invariably unquestioning) acceptance of forms into the inner meaning of which he does not greatly vex his soul by entering; nor his airy way of ridiculing what he has no intention of helping to overthrow; nor his light unconcern in the question whether he is, or is not, an immoral writer. Or, at least, in all of these things he has no share in qualities and tendencies, which influences and conflicts unknown to and unforeseen by him may be safely said to have ultimately made characteristic of Englishmen. But he *is* English in his freedom and frankness of spirit; in his manliness of mind; in his preference for the good in things as they are to the good in things as they might be; in his loyalty, his piety, his truthfulness. Of the great movement which was to mould the national character for at least a long series of generations he displays no serious foreknowledge; and of the elements already preparing to affect the course of that movement he shows a very incomplete consciousness. But of the health and strength which, after struggles many and various, made that movement possible and made it victorious, he, more than any one of his contemporaries, is the living type and the speaking witness. Thus, like the times to which he belongs, he stands half in and half out of the Middle Ages, half in and half out of a phase of our national life, which we can never hope to understand more than partially and imperfectly. And it is this, taken together with the fact that he is the first English poet to read whom is to enjoy him, and that he garnished not only our language but our literature with blossoms still adorning them in vernal freshness—which makes Chaucer's figure so unique a one in the gallery of our great English writers, and gives to his works an interest so inexhaustible for the historical as well as for the literary student.

CHAPTER II.

SOMETHING has been already said as to the conflict of opinion concerning the period of Geoffrey Chaucer's birth, the precise date of which is very unlikely ever to be ascertained. A better fortune has attended the anxious enquiries which in his case, as in those of other great men, have been directed to the very secondary question of ancestry and descent—a question to which, in the abstract at all events, no man ever attached less importance than he. Although the name *Chaucer* is (according to Thynne) to be found on the lists of Battle Abbey, this no more proves that the poet himself came of "high parage," than the reverse is to be concluded from the nature of his coat-of-arms, which Speght thought must have been taken out of the 27th and 28th Propositions of the First Book of Euclid. Many a warrior of the Norman Conquest was known to his comrades only by the name of the trade which he had plied in some French or Flemish town, before he attached himself a volunteer to Duke William's holy and lucrative expedition; and it is doubtful whether, even in the fourteenth century, the name *Le Chaucer* is, wherever it occurs in London, used as a surname, or whether, in some instances, it is not merely a designation of the owner's trade. Thus we should not be justified in

assuming a French origin for the family from which Richard le Chaucer, whom we know to have been the poet's
grandfather, was descended. Whether or not he was at
any time a shoemaker (*chaucier*, maker of *chausses*), and
accordingly belonged to a gentle craft otherwise not un-
associated with the history of poetry, Richard was a citizen of London, and vintner, like his son John after him.
John Chaucer, whose wife's Christian name may be with
tolerable safety set down as Agnes, owned a house in
Thames Street, London, not far from the arch on which
modern pilgrims pass by rail to Canterbury or beyond,
and in the neighbourhood of the great bridge, which in
Chaucer's own day emptied its travellers on their errands,
sacred or profane, into the great Southern road, the *Via
Appia* of England. The house afterwards descended to
John's son, GEOFFREY, who released his right to it by
deed in the year 1380. Chaucer's father was probably a
man of some substance, the most usual personal recom-
mendation to great people in one of his class. For he
was at least temporarily connected with the Court, inasmuch as he attended King Edward III. and Queen Philippa on the memorable journey to Flanders and Germany, in
the course of which the English monarch was proclaimed
Vicar of the Holy Roman Empire on the left bank of the
Rhine. John Chaucer died in 1366, and in course of time
his widow married another citizen and vintner. Thomas
Heyroun, John Chaucer's brother of the half-blood, was
likewise a member of the same trade ; so that the young
Geoffrey was certainly not brought up in an atmosphere
of abstinence. The *Host* of the *Canterbury Tales*, though
he takes his name from an actual personage, may therefore have in him touches of a family portrait ; but Chaucer
himself nowhere displays any traces of a hereditary devo-

tion to Bacchus, and makes so experienced a practitioner as the *Pardoner* the mouthpiece of as witty an invective against drunkenness as has been uttered by any assailant of our existing licensing laws.   Chaucer's own practice, as well as his opinion on this head, is sufficiently expressed in the characteristic words he puts into the mouth of Cressid :—

> "In everything, I wot, there lies measúre :
> For though a man forbid all drunkenness,
> He biddeth not that every créature
> Be drinkless altogether, as I guess."

Of Geoffrey Chaucer we know nothing whatever from the day of his birth (whenever it befell) to the year 1357. His earlier biographers, who supposed him to have been born in 1328, had accordingly a fair field open for conjecture and speculation.   Here it must suffice to risk the asseveration that he cannot have accompanied his father to Cologne in 1338, and on that occasion have been first "taken notice of" by king and queen, if he was not born till two or more years afterwards.   If, on the other hand, he was born in 1328, both events *may* have taken place. On neither supposition is there any reason for believing that he studied at one—or at both—of our English Universities.   The poem cannot be accepted as Chaucerian, the author of which (very possibly by a mere dramatic assumption) declares :—

> " Philogenet I call'd am far and near,
>   Of Cambridge clerk ;"

nor can any weight be attached to the circumstance that the *Clerk*, who is one of the most delightful figures among the Canterbury Pilgrims, is an Oxonian.   The enticing enquiry as to *which* of the sister Universities may claim

3*

Chaucer as her own must, therefore, be allowed to drop, together with the subsidiary question, whether stronger evidence of local colouring is furnished by the *Miller's* picture of the life of a poor scholar in lodgings at Oxford, or by the *Reeve's* rival narrative of the results of a Trumpington walk taken by two undergraduates of the "Solar Hall" at Cambridge. Equally baseless is the supposition of one of Chaucer's earliest biographers, that he completed his academical studies at Paris—and equally futile the concomitant fiction that in France " he acquired much applause by his literary exercises." Finally, we have the tradition that he was a member of the Inner Temple—which is a conclusion deduced from a piece of genial scandal as to a record having been seen in that inn of a fine imposed upon him for beating a friar in Fleet Street. This story was early placed by Thynne on the horns of a sufficiently decisive dilemma: in the days of Chaucer's youth, lawyers had not yet been admitted into the Temple; and in the days of his maturity he is not very likely to have been found engaged in battery in a London thoroughfare.

We now desert the region of groundless conjecture, in order, with the year 1357, to arrive at a firm though not very broad footing of facts. In this year "Geoffrey Chaucer" (whom it would be too great an effort of scepticism to suppose to have been merely a namesake of the poet) is mentioned in the Household Book of Elizabeth, Countess of Ulster, wife of Prince Lionel (third son of King Edward III., and afterwards Duke of Clarence), as a recipient of certain articles of apparel. Two similar notices of his name occur up to the year 1359. He is hence concluded to have belonged to Prince Lionel's establishment as squire or page to the Lady Elizabeth; and it was probably in the Prince's retinue that he took part in the

expedition of King Edward III. into France, which began
at the close of the year 1359 with the ineffectual siege of
Rheims, and in the next year, after a futile attempt upon
Paris, ended with the compromise of the Peace of Brétigny.
In the course of this campaign Chaucer was taken prison-
er; but he was released without much loss of time, as
appears by a document bearing date March 1st, 1360, in
which the King contributes the sum of 16l. for Chaucer's
ransom. We may, therefore, conclude that he missed the
march upon Paris, and the sufferings undergone by the
English army on their road thence to Chartres—the most
exciting experiences of an inglorious campaign; and that
he was actually set free by the Peace. When, in the year
1367, we next meet with his name in authentic records,
his earliest known patron, the Lady Elizabeth, is dead; and
he has passed out of the service of Prince Lionel into
that of King Edward himself, as Valet of whose Chamber
or household he receives a yearly salary for life of twenty
marks, for his former and future services. Very possibly
he had quitted Prince Lionel's service when, in 1361, that
Prince had, by reason of his marriage with the heiress of
Ulster, been appointed to the Irish government by his father, who was supposed at one time to have destined him
for the Scottish throne.

Concerning the doings of Chaucer in the interval between his liberation from his French captivity and the first
notice of him as Valet of the King's Chamber we know
nothing at all. During these years, however, no less important a personal event than his marriage was by earlier
biographers supposed to have occurred. On the other
hand, according to the view which commends itself to several eminent living commentators of the poet, it was not
courtship and marriage, but a hopeless and unrequited pas-

sion, which absorbed these years of his life. Certain stanzas in which, as they think, he gave utterance to this passion are by them ascribed to one of these years; so that,
if their view were correct, the poem in question would
have to be regarded as the earliest of his extant productions. The problem which we have indicated must detain
us for a moment.

It is attested by documentary evidence that in the year
1374 Chaucer had a wife by name Philippa, who had been
in the service of John of Gaunt, Duke of Lancaster, and
of his Duchess (doubtless his second wife, Constance), as
well as in that of his mother, the good Queen Philippa,
and who on several occasions afterwards, besides special
new-year's gifts of silver-gilt cups from the Duke, received
her annual pension of ten marks through her husband. It
is likewise proved that, in 1366, a pension of ten marks
was granted to *a* Philippa Chaucer, one of the ladies of
the Queen's Chamber. Obviously, it is a highly probable
assumption that these two Philippa Chaucers were one
and the same person; but in the absence of any direct
proof it is impossible to affirm as certain, or to deny as
demonstrably untrue, that the Philippa Chaucer of 1366
owed her surname to marriage. Yet the view was long
held, and is still maintained by writers of knowledge and
insight, that the Philippa of 1366 was at that date Chaucer's wife. In or before that year he married, it was said,
Philippa Roet, daughter of Sir Paon de Roet of Hainault,
Guienne King of Arms, who came to England in Queen
Philippa's retinue in 1328. This tradition derived special
significance from the fact that another daughter of Sir
Paon, Katharine, widow of Sir Hugh Swynford, was suc-
cessively governess, mistress, and (third) wife to the Duke
of Lancaster, to whose service both Geoffrey and Philippa

Chaucer were at one time attached. It was apparently founded on the circumstance that Thomas Chaucer, the supposed son of the poet, quartered the Roet arms with his own. But unfortunately there is no evidence to show that Thomas Chaucer was a son of Geoffrey; and the superstructure must needs vanish with its basis. It being then no longer indispensable to assume Chaucer to have been a married man in 1366, the Philippa Chaucer of that year *may* have been only a namesake, and possibly a relative, of Geoffrey; for there were other Chaucers in London besides him and his father (who died this year), and one Chaucer at least has been found who was well-to-do enough to have a Damsel of the Queen's Chamber for his daughter in these certainly not very exclusive times.

There is, accordingly, no *proof* that Chaucer was a married man before 1374, when he is known to have received a pension for his own and his wife's services. But with this negative result we are asked not to be poor-spirited enough to rest content. At the opening of his *Book of the Duchess,* a poem certainly written towards the end of the year 1369, Chaucer makes use of certain expressions, both very pathetic and very definite. The most obvious interpretation of the lines in question seems to be that they contain the confession of a hopeless passion, which has lasted for eight years — a confession which certainly seems to come more appropriately and more naturally from an unmarried than from a married man. "For eight years," he says, or seems to say, "I have loved, and loved in vain—and yet my cure is never the nearer. There is but one physician that can heal me—but all that is ended and done with. Let us pass on into fresh fields; what cannot be obtained must needs be left." It seems impossible to interpret this passage (too long to cite *in extenso*)

as a complaint of married life. Many other poets have,
indeed, complained of their married lives, and Chaucer (if
the view to be advanced below be correct) as emphatically
as any. But though such occasional exclamations of im-
patience or regret—more especially when in a comic vein
—may receive pardon, or even provoke amusement, yet a
serious and sustained poetic version of Sterne's "*sum mul-
tum fatigatus de uxore mea*" would be unbearable in any
writer of self-respect, and wholly out of character in Chaucer. Even Byron only indited elegies about his married
life after his wife *had left him*.

Now, among Chaucer's minor poems is preserved one
called the *Complaint of the Death of Pity*, which purports
to set forth "how pity is dead and buried in a gentle
heart," and, after testifying to a hopeless passion, ends
with the following declaration, addressed to Pity, as in a
"bill" or letter:—

> "This is to say: I will be yours for ever,
>   Though ye me slay by Cruelty, your foe;
>   Yet shall my spirit nevermore dissever
>   From your service, for any pain or woe,
>   Pity, whom I have sought so long ago!
>   Thus for your death I may well weep and plain,
>   With heart all sore, and full of busy pain."

If this poem be autobiographical, it would indisputably
correspond well enough to a period in Chaucer's life, and
to a mood of mind preceding those to which the introduction to the *Book of the Duchess* belongs. If it be not autobiographical—and in truth there is nothing to prove it
such, so that an attempt has been actually made to suggest
its having been intended to apply to the experiences of
another man—then the *Complaint of Pity* has no special
value for students of Chaucer, since its poetic beauty, as

there can be no harm in observing, is not in itself very great.

To come to an end of this topic, there seems no possibility of escaping from one of the following alternatives: *Either* the Philippa Chaucer of 1366 was Geoffrey Chaucer's wife, whether or not she was Philippa Roet before marriage, and the lament of 1369 had reference to another lady—an assumption to be regretted in the case of a married man, but not out of the range of possibility. *Or*—and this seems, on the whole, the most probable view —the Philippa Chaucer of 1366 was a namesake whom Geoffrey married some time after 1369 — possibly (of course only *possibly*) the very lady whom he had loved hopelessly for eight years, and persuaded himself that he had at last relinquished, and who had then relented after all. This last conjecture it is certainly difficult to reconcile with the conclusion at which we arrive on other grounds, that Chaucer's married life was not one of preponderating bliss. That he and his wife were *cousins* is a pleasing thought, but one which is not made more pleasing by the seeming fact that, if they were so related, marriage in their case failed to draw close that hearts' bond which such kinship at times half unconsciously knits.

Married or still a bachelor, Chaucer may fairly be supposed, during part of the years previous to that in which we find him securely established in the King's service, to have enjoyed a measure of independence and leisure open to few men in his rank of life, when once the golden days of youth and early manhood have passed away. Such years are in many men's lives marked by the projection, or even by the partial accomplishment, of literary undertakings on a large scale, and more especially of such as partake of an imitative character. When a juvenile and

facile writer's taste is still unsettled, and his own style is
as yet unformed, he eagerly tries his hand at the reproduction of the work of others; translates the *Iliad* or *Faust*,
or suits himself with unsuspecting promptitude to the production of masques, or pastorals, or life dramas—or whatever may be the prevailing fashion in poetry—after the
manner of the favourite literary models of the day. *A priori*, therefore, everything is in favour of the belief hitherto
universally entertained, that among Chaucer's earliest poetical productions was the extant English translation of
the French *Roman de la Rose*. That he made *some* translation of this poem is a fact resting on his own statement
in a passage indisputably written by him (in the *Prologue*
to the *Legend of Good Women*); nor is the value of this
statement reduced by the negative circumstance, that in
the extraordinary tag (if it may be called by so irreverent
a name) to the extant *Canterbury Tales*, the *Romaunt of
the Rose* is passed over in silence, or at least not nominally
mentioned, among the objectionable works which the poet
is there made to retract. And there seems at least no necessity for giving in to the conclusion that Chaucer's translation has been lost, and was not that which has been hitherto accepted as his. For this conclusion is based upon
the use of a formal test, which, in truth, need not be regarded as of itself absolutely decisive in any case, but
which in this particular instance need not be held applica-
ble at all. A particular rule against rhyming with one another particular sounds, which in his later poems Chaucer
seems invariably to have followed, need not have been observed by him in what was actually, or all but, his earliest.
The unfinished state of the extant translation accords with
the supposition that Chaucer broke it off on adopting (possibly after conference with Gower, who likewise observes

the rule) a more logical practice as to the point in question. Moreover, no English translation of this poem besides Chaucer's is ever known to have existed.

Whither should the youthful poet, when in search of materials on which to exercise a ready but as yet untrained hand, have so naturally turned as to French poetry, and in its domain whither so eagerly as to its universally acknowledged master-piece? French verse was the delight of the Court, into the service of which he was about this time preparing permanently to enter, and with which he had been more or less connected from his boyhood. In French, Chaucer's contemporary Gower composed not only his first longer work, but not less than fifty ballads or sonnets; and in French (as well as in English) Chaucer himself may have possibly in his youth set his own 'prentice hand to the turning of "*ballades, rondels, virelayes.*" The time had not yet arrived, though it was not far distant, when his English verse was to attest his admiration of Machault, whose fame Froissart and Froissart's imitations had brought across from the French Court to the English, and when Gransson, who served King Richard II. as a squire, was extolled by his English adapter as the "flower of them that write in France." But as yet Chaucer's own tastes, his French blood, if he had any in his veins, and the familiarity with the French tongue which he had already had opportunities of acquiring, were more likely to commend to him productions of broader literary merits and a wider popularity. From these points of view, in the days of Chaucer's youth, there was no rival to the *Roman de la Rose*, one of those rare works on which the literary history of whole generations and centuries may be said to hinge. The Middle Ages, in which, from various causes, the literary intercommunication between the

nations of Europe was in some respects far livelier than it
has been in later times, witnessed the appearance of several
such works—diverse in kind, but similar to one another
in the universality of their popularity : the *Consolation of
Philosophy*, the *Divine Comedy*, the *Imitation of Christ*,
the *Roman de la Rose*, the *Ship of Fools*. The favour enjoyed by the *Roman de la Rose* was in some ways the
most extraordinary of all. In France, this work remained
the dominant work of poetic literature, and "the source
whence every rhymer drew for his needs" down to the
period of the classical revival led by Ronsard (when it was
edited by Clement Marot, Spenser's early model). In England, it exercised an influence only inferior to that which
belonged to it at home upon both the matter and the
form of poetry down to the renascence begun by Surrey
and Wyatt. This extraordinary literary influence admits
of a double explanation. But just as the authorship of
the poem was very unequally divided between two personages, wholly divergent in their purposes as writers, so the
popularity of the poem is probably in the main to be attributed to the second and later of the pair.

To the *trouvère* Guillaume de Lorris (who took his
name from a small town in the valley of the Loire) was
due the original conception of the *Roman de la Rose*, for
which it is needless to suspect any extraneous source. To
novelty of subject he added great ingenuity of treatment.
Instead of a narrative of warlike adventures he offered to
his readers a psychological romance, in which a combina-
tion of symbolisations and personified abstractions supplied
the characters of the moral conflict represented. Bestiaries
and Lapidaries had familiarised men's minds with the art
of finding a symbolical significance in particular animals
and stones; and the language of poets was becoming a

language of flowers. On the other hand, the personifica-
tion of abstract qualities was a usage largely affected by
the Latin writers of the earlier Middle Ages, and formed a
favourite device of the monastic beginnings of the Christian drama. For both these literary fashions, which mildly exercised the ingenuity while deeply gratifying the
tastes of mediæval readers, room was easily found by
Guillaume de Lorris within a framework in itself both appropriate and graceful. He told (as reproduced by his
English translator) how in a dream he seemed to himself
to wake up on a May morning. Sauntering forth, he
came to a garden surrounded by a wall, on which were
depicted many unkindly figures, such as Hate and Villainy,
and Avarice and Old Age, and another thing

> "That seemèd like a hypocrite,
> And it was clepèd pope holy."

Within, all seemed so delicious that, feeling ready to give
an hundred pound for the chance of entering, he smote at
a small wicket, and was admitted by a courteous maiden
named Idleness. On the sward in the garden were dancing its owner, Sir Mirth, and a company of friends; and
by the side of Gladness the dreamer saw the God of Love
and his attendant, a bachelor named Sweet-looking, who
bore two bows, each with five arrows. Of these bows the
one was straight and fair, and the other crooked and un-
sightly, and each of the arrows bore the name of some
quality or emotion by which love is advanced or hindered.
And as the dreamer was gazing into the spring of Narcis-
sus (the imagination), he beheld a rose-tree "charged full
of roses," and, becoming enamoured of one of them, eagerly advanced to pluck the object of his passion. In the
midst of this attempt he was struck by arrow upon arrow,

shot "wonder smart" by Love from the strong bow. The
arrow called Company completes the victory; the dream-
ing poet becomes the Lover (*L'Amant*), and swears alle-
giance to the God of Love, who proceeds to instruct him
in his laws; and the real action (if it is to be called such)
of the poem begins. This consists in the Lover's desire
to possess himself of the Rosebud, the opposition offered
to him by powers both good and evil, and by Reason in
particular, and the support which he receives from more
or less discursive friends. Clearly, the conduct of such a
scheme as this admits of being varied in many ways and
protracted to any length; but its first conception is easy
and natural, and, when it was novel to boot, was neither
commonplace nor ill-chosen.

After writing about one-fifth of the 22,000 verses of
which the original French poem consists, Guillaume de
Lorris, who had executed his part of the task in full sympathy with the spirit of the chivalry of his times, died,
and left the work to be continued by another *trouvère*,
Jean de Meung (so-called from the town, near Lorris, in
which he lived). "Hobbling John" took up the thread
of his predecessor's poem in the spirit of a wit and an
encyclopædist. Indeed, the latter appellation suits him
in both its special and its general sense. Beginning with
a long dialogue between Reason and the Lover, he was
equally anxious to display his freedom of criticism and
his universality of knowledge, both scientific and anecdot-
ical. His vein was pre-eminently satirical and abundantly
allusive; and among the chief objects of his satire are the
two favourite themes of mediæval satire in general, religious hypocrisy (personified in *Faux-Semblant*, who has
been described as one of the ancestors of *Tartuffe*), and
the foibles of women. To the gross salt of Jean de Meung,

even more than to the courtly perfume of Guillaume de
Lorris, may be ascribed the long-lived popularity of the
Roman de la Rose; and thus a work, of which already
the theme and first conception imply a great step forwards from the previous range of mediæval poetry, became a favourite with all classes by reason of the piquancy
of its flavour, and the quotable applicability of many of
its passages. Out of a chivalrous allegory Jean de Meung
had made a popular satire; and though in its completed
form it could look for no welcome in many a court or
castle — though Petrarch despised it, and Gerson, in the
name of the Church, recorded a protest against it—and
though a bevy of offended ladies had well-nigh taken the
law into their own hands against its author—yet it commanded a vast public of admirers. And against such a
popularity even an offended clergy, though aided by the
sneers of the fastidious and the vehemence of the fair, is
wont to contend in vain.

Chaucer's translation of this poem is thought to have
been the cause which called forth from Eustace Des-
champs, Machault's pupil and nephew, the complimentary *ballade* in the refrain of which the Englishman is
saluted as

" Grant translateur, noble Geffroi Chaucier."

But whether or not such was the case, his version of the
Roman de la Rose seems, on the whole, to be a translation
properly so called—although, considering the great number of MSS. existing of the French original, it would
probably be no easy task to verify the assertion that in
one or the other of these are to be found the few passages
thought to have been interpolated by Chaucer. On the
other hand, his omissions are extensive; indeed, the whole

of his translation amounts to little more than one-third of
the French original. It is all the more noteworthy that
Chaucer reproduces only about one-half of the part contributed by Jean de Meung, and again condenses this half
to one-third of its length. In general, he has preserved
the French names of localities, and even occasionally helps
himself to a rhyme by retaining a French word. Occasionally he shows a certain timidity as a translator, speaking of "the tree which in France men call a pine," and
pointing out, so that there may be no mistake, that mer-
maidens are called "sereyns" (*sirènes*) in France. On the
other hand, his natural vivacity now and then suggests to
him a turn of phrase or an illustration of his own. As a
loyal English courtier he cannot compare a fair bachelor
to any one so aptly as to "the lord's son of Windsor;"
and as writing not far from the time when the Statute of
Kilkenny was passed, he cannot lose the opportunity of
inventing an Irish parentage for Wicked-Tongue:

> "So full of cursèd rage
> It well agreed with his lineáge;
> For him an Irishwoman bare."

The debt which Chaucer in his later works owed to the
Roman of the Rose was considerable, and by no means
confined to the favourite May-morning exordium and
the recurring machinery of a vision — to the origin of
which latter (the dream of Scipio related by Cicero and
expounded in the widely-read Commentary of Macrobius)
the opening lines of the *Romaunt* point. He owes to the
French poem both the germs of felicitous phrases, such
as the famous designation of Nature as "the Vicar of the
Almighty Lord," and perhaps touches used by him in
passages like that in which he afterwards, with further

aid from other sources, drew the character of a true gentleman. But the main service which the work of this
translation rendered to him was the opportunity which it
offered of practising and perfecting a ready and happy
choice of words — a service in which, perhaps, lies the
chief use of all translation, considered as an exercise of
style. How far he had already advanced in this respect,
and how lightly our language was already moulding itself
in his hands, may be seen from several passages in the
poem; for instance, from that about the middle, where
the old and new theme of self-contradictoriness of love is
treated in endless variations. In short, Chaucer executed
his task with facility, and frequently with grace, though,
for one reason or another, he grew tired of it before he
had carried it out with completeness. Yet the translation
(and this may have been among the causes why he seems
to have wearied of it) has, notwithstanding, a certain air
of schoolwork; and though Chaucer's next poem, to which
incontestable evidence assigns the date of the year 1369,
is still very far from being wholly original, yet the step is
great from the *Romaunt of the Rose* to the *Book of the
Duchess*.

Among the passages of the French *Roman de la Rose*
omitted in Chaucer's translation are some containing critical reflexions on the character of kings and constituted
authorities — a species of observations which kings and
constituted authorities have never been notorious for loving. This circumstance, together with the reference to
Windsor quoted above, suggests the probability that Chaucer's connexion with the Court had not been interrupted,
or had been renewed, or was on the eve of renewing itself,
at the time when he wrote this translation. In becoming
a courtier, he was certainly placed within the reach of so-

cial opportunities such as in his day he could nowhere else
have enjoyed.   In England as well as in Italy, during the
fourteenth and the two following centuries, as the frequent
recurrence of the notion attests, the "good" courtier seemed the perfection of the idea of gentleman.   At the same
time, exaggerated conceptions of the courtly breeding of
Chaucer's and Froissart's age may very easily be formed;
and it is almost amusing to contrast with Chaucer's generally liberal notions of manners, severe views of etiquette
like that introduced by him at the close of the *Man of
Law's Tale*, where he stigmatizes as a solecism the statement of the author from whom he copied his narrative,
that King Ælla sent his little boy to invite the emperor
to dinner.   "It is best to deem he went himself."

The position which in June, 1367, we find Chaucer
holding at Court is that of "Valettus" to the King, or,
as a later document of May, 1368, has it, of "Valettus
Cameræ Regis"—Valet or Yeoman of the King's Chamber.   Posts of this kind, which involved the ordinary functions of personal attendance—the making of beds, the
holding of torches, the laying of tables, the going on mes-
sages, etc.—were usually bestowed upon young men of
good family.   In due course of time a royal valet usually
rose to the higher post of royal squire—either "of the
household" generally, or of a more special kind.   Chaucer
appears in 1368 as an "esquire of less degree," his name
standing seventeenth in a list of seven-and-thirty.   After
the year 1373 he is never mentioned by the lower, but several times by Latin equivalents of the higher, title.   Frequent entries occur of the pension or salary of twenty
marks granted to him for life; and, as will be seen, he
soon began to be employed on missions abroad.   He had
thus become a regular member of the royal establishment,

within the sphere of which we must suppose the associations of the next years of his life to have been confined. They belonged to a period of peculiar significance both for the English people and for the Plantagenet dynasty, whose glittering exploits reflected so much transitory glory on the national arms. At home, these years were the brief interval between two of the chief visitations of the Black Death (1361 and 1369); and a few years earlier the poet of the *Vision* had given voice to the sufferings of the poor. It was not, however, the mothers of the people crying for their children whom the courtly singer remembered in his elegy written in the year 1369; the woe to which he gave a poetic expression was that of a princely widower temporarily inconsolable for the loss of his first wife. In 1367 the Black Prince was conquering Castile (to be lost again before the year was out) for that interesting protégé of the Plantagenets and representative of legitimate right, Don Pedro the Cruel, whose daughter the inconsolable widower was to espouse in 1372, and whose "tragic" downfall Chaucer afterwards duly lamented in his *Monk's Tale*:—

> "O noble, O worthy Pedro, glory of Spain,
> Whom fortune held so high in majesty!"

As yet the star of the valiant Prince of Wales had not been quenched in the sickness which was the harbinger of death; and his younger brother, John of Gaunt, though already known for his bravery in the field (he commanded the reinforcements sent to Spain in 1367), had scarcely begun to play the prominent part in politics which he was afterwards to fill. But his day was at hand, and the anti-clerical tenour of the legislation and of the administrative changes of these years was in entire harmony with the policy of which he was to constitute himself the represent-

4

ative. 1365 is the year of the Statute of Provisors, and
1371 that of the dismissal of William of Wykeham.

John of Gaunt was born in 1340, and was, therefore,
probably of much the same age as Chaucer, and, like him,
now in the prime of life. Nothing could, accordingly, be
more natural than that a more or less intimate relation
should have formed itself between them. This relation,
there is reason to believe, afterwards ripened, on Chaucer's part, into one of distinct political partisanship, of
which there could as yet (for the reason given above)
hardly be a question. There was, however, so far as we
know, nothing in Chaucer's tastes and tendencies to render
it antecedently unlikely that he should have been ready to
follow the fortunes of a prince who entered the political
arena as an adversary of clerical predominance. Had
Chaucer been a friend of it in principle, he would hardly
have devoted his first efforts as a writer to the translation
of the *Roman de la Rose*. In so far, therefore—and in
truth it is not very far—as John of Gaunt may be afterwards said to have been a Wycliffite, the same description
might probably be applied to Chaucer. With such sentiments a personal orthodoxy was fully reconcileable in both
patron and follower; and the so-called *Chaucer's A. B. C.*,
a version of a prayer to the Virgin in a French poetical
" Pilgrimage," might with equal probability have been put
together by him either early or late in the course of his
life. There was, however, a tradition, repeated by Speght,
that this piece was composed " at the request of Blanche,
Duchess of Lancaster, as a prayer for her private use, being a woman in her religion very devout." If so, it must
have been written before the Duchess's death, which occurred in 1369 ; and we may imagine it, if we please, with
its twenty-three initial letters blazoned in red and blue and

gold on a flyleaf inserted in the Book of the pious Duchess—herself, in the fervent language of the poem, an illuminated calendar, as being lighted in this world with the Virgin's holy name.

In the autumn of 1369, then, the Duchess Blanche died an early death; and it is pleasing to know that John of Gaunt, to whom his marriage with her had brought wealth and a dukedom, ordered services, in pious remembrance of her, to be held at her grave. The elaborate elegy which— very possibly at the widowed Duke's request—was composed by Chaucer, leaves no doubt as to the identity of the lady whose loss it deplores :—

> "... Goodë fairë *White* she hight ;
> Thus was my lady namèd right ;
> For she was both fair and bright."

But, in accordance with the taste of his age, which shunned such sheer straightforwardness in poetry, the *Book of the Duchess* contains no further transparent reference to the actual circumstances of the wedded life which had come to so premature an end — for John of Gaunt had married Blanche of Lancaster in 1359 — and an elaborate framework is constructed round the essential theme of the poem. Already, however, the instinct of Chaucer's own poetic genius had taught him the value of personal directness; and, artificially as the course of the poem is arranged, it begins in the most artless and effective fashion with an account given by the poet of his own sleeplessness and its cause, already referred to—an opening so felicitous that it was afterwards imitated by Froissart. And so, Chaucer continues, as he could not sleep, to drive the night away he sat upright in his bed reading a "romance," which he thought better entertainment than chess or draughts. The book which he read was the *Metamor-phoses* of Ovid ; and in it he chanced on the tale of Ceyx and Alcyone—the lovers whom, on their premature death, the compassion of Juno changed into the sea-birds that bring good-luck to mariners. Of this story (whether Chaucer derived it direct from Ovid, or from Machault's French version, is disputed), the earlier part serves as the introduction to the poem. The story breaks off — with the dramatic abruptness in which Chaucer is a master, and which so often distinguishes his versions from their orig-inals—at the death of Alcyone, caused by her grief at the tidings brought by Morpheus of her husband's death. Thus subtly the god of sleep and the death of a loving wife mingle their images in the poet's mind ; and with these upon him, he falls asleep " right upon his book."

What more natural, after this, than the dream which came to him? It was May, and he lay in his bed at morn-ing-time, having been awakened out of his slumbers by the " small-fowls," who were carolling forth their notes— " some high, some low, and all of one accord." The birds singing their matins around the poet, and the sun shining brightly through his windows stained with many a figure of poetic legend, and upon the walls painted in fine colours, "both text and gloss, and all the Rómaunt of the Rose"— is not this a picture of Chaucer by his own hand, on which one may love to dwell?   And just as the poem has begun with a touch of nature, and at the beginning of its main action has returned to nature, so through the whole of its course it maintains the same tone.   The sleeper awakened —still, of course, in his dream — hears the sound of the horn, and the noise of huntsmen preparing for the chase. He rises, saddles his horse, and follows to the forest, where the Emperor Octavian (a favourite character of Carolingian legend, and pleasantly revived under this aspect by the modern romanticist, Ludwig Tieck — in Chaucer's poem probably a flattering allegory for the King) is holding his hunt. The deer having been started, the poet is watching the course of the hunt, when he is approached by a dog, which leads him to a solitary spot in a thicket among mighty trees; and here of a sudden he comes upon a man in black, sitting silently by the side of a huge oak. How simple and how charming is the device of the faithful dog acting as a guide into the mournful solitude of the faithful man ! For the knight whom the poet finds thus silent and alone, is rehearsing to himself a lay, "a manner song," in these words :—

> "I have of sorrow so great wone,
>   That joyë get I never none,
>   Now that I see my lady bright,
>   Which I have loved with all my might,
>   Is from me dead, and is agone.
>   Alas ! Death, what aileth thee
>   That thou should'st not have taken me,
>   When that thou took'st my lady sweet ?
>   That was so fair, so fresh, so free,
>   So goodë, that men may well see
>   Of all goodnéss she had no meet."

Seeing the knight overcome by his grief, and on the point of fainting, the poet accosts him, and courteously demands his pardon for the intrusion. Thereupon the disconsolate mourner, touched by this token of sympathy, breaks out into the tale of his sorrow which forms the real subject of the poem. It is a lament for the loss of a wife who was hard to gain (the historical basis of this is unknown, but great heiresses are usually hard to gain for cadets even of royal houses), and whom, alas ! her husband was to lose so soon after he had gained her. Nothing could be simpler, and nothing could be more delightful, than the Black Knight's description of his lost lady as she was at the time when he wooed and almost despaired of winning her. Many of the touches in this description—and among them some of the very happiest—are, it is true, borrowed from the courtly Machault; but nowhere has Chaucer been happier, both in his appropriations and in the way in which he has really converted them into beauties of his own, than in this, perhaps the most lifelike picture of maidenhood in the whole range of our literature. Or is not the following the portrait of an English girl, all life and all innocence—a type not belonging, like its opposite, to any " period " in particular?

> " I saw her dance so comelily,
> Carol and sing so sweetëly,
> And laugh, and play so womanly,
> And lookë so debónairly,
> So goodly speak and so friendlÿ,
> That, certes, I trow that nevermore
> Was seen so blissful a treasúre.
> For every hair upon her head,
> Sooth to say, it was not red,
> Nor yellow neither, nor brown it was,
> Methought most likë gold it was.
> And ah! what eyes my lady had,
> Debónair, goodë, glad and sad,
> Simple, of good size, not too wide.
> Thereto her look was not aside,
> Nor overthwart ;"

but so well set that whoever beheld her was drawn and taken up by it, every part of him. Her eyes seemed every now and then as if she were inclined to be merciful, such was the delusion of fools : a delusion in very truth, for

> " It was no counterfeited thing ;
> It was her ownë pure looking ;
> So the goddess, dame Natúre,
> Had made them open by measúre
> And close ; for were she never so glad,
> Not foolishly her looks were spread,
> Nor wildëly, though that she play'd ;
> But ever, methought, her eyen said,
> 'By God, my wrath is all forgiven.' "

And at the same time she liked to live so happily that
dulness was afraid of her ; she was neither too "sober"
nor too glad ; in short, no creature had ever more measure
in all things. Such was the lady whom the knight had
won for himself, and whose virtues he cannot weary of rehearsing to himself or to a sympathising auditor.

> " 'Sir !' quoth I, 'where is she now ?'
> 'Now ?' quoth he, and stopped anon ;
> Therewith he waxed as dead as stone,
> And said : 'Alas that I was bore !
> That was the loss ! and heretofore
> I told to thee what I had lost.
> Bethink thee what I said.   Thou know'st
> In sooth full little what thou meanest :
> I have lost morë than thou weenest.
> God wot, alas ! right that was she.'
> 'Alas, sir, how ? what may that be ?'
> 'She is dead.'   'Nay ?'   'Yes, by my truth !'
> 'Is that your loss ? by God, it is ruth.' "

And with that word, the hunt breaking up, the knight
and the poet depart to a "long castle with white walls on
a rich hill" (Richmond ?), where a bell tolls and awakens
the poet from his slumbers, to let him find himself lying
in his bed, and the book, with its legend of love and sleep,
resting in his hand.   One hardly knows at whom more to

wonder—whether at the distinguished French scholar who
sees so many trees that he cannot see a forest, and who,
not content with declaring the *Book of the Duchess*, as a
whole as well as in its details, a servile imitation of Machault, pronounces it at the same time one of Chaucer's
feeblest productions; or at the equally eminent English
scholar who, with a flippancy which for once ceases to be
amusing, opines that Chaucer ought to " have felt ashamed
of himself for this most lame and impotent conclusion"
of a poem " full of beauties," and ought to have been
" caned for it !" Not only was this " lame and impotent
conclusion" imitated by Spenser in his lovely elegy, *Daphnaïda ;*[1] but it is the first passage in Chaucer's writings
revealing, one would have thought unmistakeably, the dramatic power which was among his most characteristic gifts.
The charm of this poem, notwithstanding all the artificialities with which it is overlaid, lies in its simplicity and
truth to nature. A real human being is here brought before us instead of a vague abstraction ; and the glow of
life is on the page, though it has to tell of death and
mourning. Chaucer is finding his strength by dipping
into the true spring of poetic inspiration ; and in his
dreams he is awaking to the real capabilities of his genius.
Though he is still uncertain of himself and dependent on
others, it seems not too much to say that already in this

---

[1] I have been anticipated in pointing out this fact by the author
of the biographical essay on *Spenser* in this series—an essay to which
I cannot help taking this opportunity of offering a tribute of sincere
admiration. It may not be an undesigned coincidence that the inconsolable widower of the *Daphnaïda* is named Alcyon, while Chaucer's poem begins with a reference to the myth of Ceyx and Alcyone.
Sir Arthur Gorges reappears as Alcyon in *Colin Clout's come home
again.*

Book of the Duchess he is in some measure an original poet.

How unconscious, at the same time, this waking must have been is manifest from what little is known concerning the course of both his personal and his literary life during the next few years. But there is a tide in the lives of poets, as in those of other men, on the use or neglect of which their future seems largely to depend. For more reasons than one, Chaucer may have been rejoiced to be employed on the two missions abroad, which apparently formed his chief occupation during the years 1370–1373. In the first place, the love of books, which he so frequently confesses, must in him have been united to a love of seeing men and cities; few are observers of character without taking pleasure in observing it. Of his literary labours he probably took little thought during these years; although the visit which in the course of them he paid to Italy may be truly said to have constituted the turning-point in his literary life. No work of his can be ascribed to this period with certainty; none of importance has ever been ascribed to it.

On the latter of these missions Chaucer, who left England in the winter of 1372, visited Genoa and Florence. His object at the former city was to negotiate concerning the settlement of a Genoese mercantile factory in one of our ports, for in this century there already existed between Genoa and England a commercial intercourse, which is illustrated by the obvious etymology of the popular term *jane* occurring in Chaucer in the sense of any small coin.[1] It has been supposed that on this journey he met at Padua

---

[1] "A jane" is in the *Clerk's Tale* said to be a sufficient value at which to estimate the "stormy people."

4*

Petrarch, whose residence was near by at Arqua. The
statement of the *Clerk* in the *Canterbury Tales* that he
learnt the story of patient Griseldis " at Padua of a worthy
clerk . . . now dead," who was called " Francis Petrarch,
the laureate poet," may, of course, merely imply that Chaucer borrowed the *Clerk's Tale* from Petrarch's Latin version of the original by Boccaccio.   But the meeting which
the expression suggests may have actually taken place, and
may have been accompanied by the most suitable conversation which the imagination can supply; while, on the
other hand, it is a conjecture unsupported by any evidence
whatever, that a previous meeting between the pair had
occurred at Milan in 1368, when Lionel, Duke of Clarence,
was married to his second wife with great pomp in the
presence of Petrarch and of Froissart.   The really noteworthy point is this: that while neither (as a matter of
course) the translated *Romaunt of the Rose* nor the *Book
of the Duchess* exhibits any traces of Italian influence, the
same assertion cannot safely be made with regard to any
important poem produced by Chaucer after the date of
this Italian journey.   The literature of Italy, which was—
and in the first instance through Chaucer himself—to exercise so powerful an influence upon the progress of our
own, was at last opened to him, though in what measure,
and by what gradations, must remain undecided.   Before
him lay both the tragedies and the comedies, as he would
have called them, of the learned and brilliant Boccaccio—
both his epic poems and that inexhaustible treasure-house
of stories which Petrarch praised for its pious and grave
contents, albeit they were mingled with others of undeniable jocoseness—the immortal *Decamerone*.   He could ex-
amine the refined gold of Petrarch's own verse, with its
exquisite variations of its favourite pure theme and its ad-

equate treatment of other elevated subjects; and he might gaze down the long vista of pictured reminiscences, grand and sombre, called up by the mightiest Muse of the Middle Ages, the Muse of Dante. Chaucer's genius, it may be said at once, was not *transformed* by its contact with Italian literature; for a conscious desire as well as a conscientious effort is needed for bringing about such a transformation; and to compare the results of his first Italian journey with those of Goethe's pilgrimage across the Alps, for instance, would be palpably absurd. It might even be doubted whether, for the themes which he was afterwards likely to choose, and actually did choose, for poetic treatment, the materials at his command in French (and English) poetry and prose would not have sufficed him. As it was, it seems probable that he took many things from Italian literature; it is certain that he learnt much from it. There seems every reason to conclude that the influence of Italian study upon Chaucer made him more assiduous, as well as more careful, in the employment of his poetic powers—more hopeful at once, if one may so say, and more assured of himself.

Meanwhile, soon after his return from his second foreign mission, he was enabled to begin a more settled life at home. He had acquitted himself to the satisfaction of the Crown, as is shown by the grant for life of a daily pitcher of wine, made to him on April 23rd, 1374, the merry day of the Feast of St. George. It would, of course, be a mistake to conclude, from any seeming analogies of later times, that this grant, which was received by Chaucer in money-value, and which seems finally to have been commuted for an annual payment of twenty marks, betokened on the part of the King a spirit of patronage appropriate to the claims of literary leisure. How remote such a no-

tion was from the minds of Chaucer's employers is proved
by the terms of the patent by which, in the month of June
following, he was appointed Comptroller of the Customs
and Subsidy of wools, skins, and tanned hides in the port
of London. This patent (doubtless according to the usual
official form) required him to write the rolls of his office
with his own hand, to be continually present there, and to
perform his duties in person, and not by deputy. By a war-
rant of the same month Chaucer was granted the pension
of 10*l.* for life already mentioned, for services rendered by
him and his wife to the Duke and Duchess of Lancaster
and to the Queen ; by two successive grants of the year
1375 he received further pecuniary gratifications of a more
or less temporary nature ; and he continued to receive his
pension and allowance for robes as one of the royal es-
quires. We may, therefore, conceive of him as now established in a comfortable as well as seemingly secure position. His regular work as comptroller (of which a few
scattered documentary vestiges are preserved) scarcely offers more points for the imagination to exercise itself upon
than Burns's excisemanship or Wordsworth's collectorship
of stamps,[1] though doubtless it must have brought him
into constant contact with merchants and with shipmen,
and may have suggested to him many a broad descriptive
touch. On the other hand, it is not necessary to be a poet
to feel something of that ineffable *ennui* of official life, which
even the self-compensatory practice of arriving late at one's
desk, but departing from it early, can only abate, but not
take away. The passage has been often quoted in which
Chaucer half implies a feeling of the kind, and tells how

[1] It is a curious circumstance that Dryden should have received,
as a reward for his political services as a satirist, an office almost
identical with Chaucer's. But he held it for little more than a year.

he sought recreation from what Charles Lamb would have
called his "works" at the Custom House in the reading,
as we know he did in the writing, of other books:—

> " . . . When thy labour done all is,
> And hast y-madë reckonings,
> Instead of rest and newë things
> Thou go'st home to thine house anon,
> And there as dumb as any stone
> Thou sittest at another book."

The house at home was doubtless that in Aldgate, of which
the lease to Chaucer, bearing date May, 1374, has been discovered; and to this we may fancy Chaucer walking morning and evening from the river-side, past the Postern Gate
by the Tower.   Already, however, in 1376, the routine of
his occupations appears to have been interrupted by his
engagement on some secret service under Sir John Bur-
ley; and in the following year, and in 1378, he was repeatedly abroad in the service of the Crown.   On one of
his journeys in the last-named year he was attached in a
subordinate capacity to the embassy sent to negotiate for
the marriage with the French King Charles V.'s daughter
Mary to the young King Richard II., who had succeeded
to his grandfather in 1377 — one of those matrimonial
missions which, in the days of both Plantagenets and Tu-
dors, formed so large a part of the functions of European
diplomacy, and which not unfrequently, as in this case at
least ultimately, came to nothing.   A later journey in May
of the same year took Chaucer once more to Italy, whither
he had been sent with Sir Edward Berkeley to treat with
Bernardo Visconti, joint lord of Milan, and "scourge of
Lombardy," and Sir John Hawkwood — the former of
whom finds a place in that brief mirror of magistrates,
the *Monk's Tale*.   It was on this occasion that of the two

persons whom, according to custom, Chaucer appointed to appear for him in the Courts during his absence, one was John Gower, whose name as that of the second poet of his age is indissolubly linked with Chaucer's own.

So far, the new reign, which had opened amidst doubts and difficulties for the country, had to the faithful servant of the dynasty brought an increase of royal good-will. In 1381—after the suppression of the great rebellion of the villeins—King Richard II. had married the princess whose name for a season linked together the history of two countries the destinies of which had before that age, as they have since, lain far asunder. Yet both Bohemia and England, besides the nations which received from the former the impulses communicated to it by the latter, have reason to remember Queen Anne, the learned and the good; since to her was probably due, in the first instance, the intellectual intercourse between her native and her adopted country. There seems every reason to believe that it was the approach of this marriage which Chaucer celebrated in one of the brightest and most jocund marriage-poems ever composed by a laureate's hand; and if this was so, he cannot but have augmented the favour with which he was regarded at Court. When, therefore, by May, 1382, his foreign journeys had come to an end, we do not wonder to find that, without being called upon to relinquish his former office, he was appointed in addition to the Comptrollership of the Petty Customs in the Port of London, of which post he was allowed to execute the duties by deputy. In November, 1384, he received permission to absent himself from his old comptrollership for a month; and in February, 1385, was allowed to appoint a (permanent) deputy for this office also. During the month of October, 1386, he sat in Parliament at Westminster as one of the Knights of the Shire for Kent, where we may consequently assume him to have possessed landed property. His fortunes, therefore, at this period had clearly risen to their height; and naturally enough his commentators are anxious to assign to these years the sunniest, as well as some of the most elaborate, of his literary productions. It is altogether probable that the amount of leisure now at Chaucer's command enabled him to carry into execution some of the works for which he had gathered materials abroad and at home, and to prepare others. Inasmuch as it contains the passage cited above, referring to Chaucer's official employment, his poem called the *House of Fame* must have been written between 1374 and 1386 (when Chaucer quitted office), and probably is to be dated near the latter year. Inasmuch as both this poem and *Troilus and Cressid* are mentioned in the Prologue to the *Legend of Good Women*, they must have been written earlier than it; and the dedication of *Troilus* to Gower and Strode very well agrees with the relations known to have existed about this time between Chaucer and his brother-poet. Very probably all these three works may have been put forth, in more or less rapid succession, during this fortunate season of Chaucer's life.

A fortunate season — for in it the prince who, from whatever cause, was indisputably the patron of Chaucer and his wife, had, notwithstanding his unpopularity among the lower orders, and the deep suspicion fostered by hostile whisperings against him in his royal nephew's breast, still contrived to hold the first place by the throne. Though serious danger had already existed of a conflict between the King and his uncle, yet John of Gaunt and his Duchess Constance had been graciously dismissed with a royal gift of golden crowns, when, in July, 1386, he

took his departure for the Continent, to busy himself till
his return home in November, 1389, with the affairs of
Castile, and with claims arising out of his disbursements
there. The reasons for Chaucer's attachment to this particular patron are probably not far to seek; on the precise
nature of the relation between them it is useless to specu-
late. Before Wyclif's death in 1384, John of Gaunt had
openly dissociated himself from the reformer; and whatever may have been the case in his later years, it was
certainly not as a follower of his old patron that at this
date Chaucer could have been considered a Wycliffite.

Again, this period of Chaucer's life may be called fortunate, because during it he seems to have enjoyed the
only congenial friendships of which any notice remains to
us. The poem of *Troilus and Cressid* is, as was just noted,
dedicated to "the moral Gower and the philosophical
Strode." Ralph Strode was a Dominican of Jedburgh
Abbey, a travelled scholar, whose journeys had carried
him as far as the Holy Land, and who was celebrated as
a poet in both the Latin and the English tongue, and as
a theologian and philosopher. In connexion with speculations concerning Chaucer's relations to Wycliffism it is
worth noting that Strode, who, after his return to England,
was appointed to superintend several new monasteries,
was the author of a series of controversial arguments
against Wyclif. The tradition, according to which he
taught one of Chaucer's sons, is untrustworthy. Of John
Gower's life little more is known than of Chaucer's; he
appears to have been a Suffolk man, holding manors in
that county as well as in Essex, but occasionally to have
resided in Kent. At the period of which we are speaking, he may be supposed, besides his French productions,
to have already published his Latin *Vox Clamantis* — a

poem which, beginning with an allegorical narrative of
Wat Tyler's rebellion, passes on to a series of reflexions
on the causes of the movement, conceived in a spirit of
indignation against the corruptions of the Church, but
not of sympathy with Wycliffism. This is no doubt the
poem which obtained for Gower the epithet "moral"
(*i. e.*, sententious) applied to him by Chaucer, and afterwards by Dunbar, Hawes, and Shakspeare. Gower's *Vox
Clamantis* and other Latin poems (including one "against
the astuteness of the Evil One in the matter of Lollardry")
are forgotten; but his English *Confessio Amantis* has retained its right to a place of honour in the history of
our literature. The most interesting part of this poem,
its *Prologue*, has already been cited as of value for our
knowledge of the political and social condition of its
times. It gives expression to a conservative tone and tem-
per of mind; and, like many conservative minds, Gower's
had adopted, or affected to adopt, the conviction that the
world was coming to an end. The cause of the anticipated catastrophe he found in the division, or absence of
concord and love, manifest in the condition of things
around. The intensity of strife visible among the con-
flicting elements of which the world, like the individual
human being, is composed, too clearly announced the
imminent end of all things. Would that a new Arion
might arise to make peace where now is hate; but,
alas! the prevailing confusion is such that God alone
may set it right. But the poem which follows cannot
be said to sustain the interest excited by this introduction. Its machinery was obviously suggested by that
of the *Roman de la Rose*, though, as Warton has happily phrased it, Gower, after a fashion of his own, blends
Ovid's *Art of Love* with the Breviary. The poet, wander-

ing about in a forest, while suffering under the smart of
Cupid's dart, meets Venus, the Goddess of Love, who urges
him, as one upon the point of death, to make his full confession to her clerk or priest, the holy father Genius. This
confession hereupon takes place by means of question and
answer; both penitent and confessor entering at great
length into an examination of the various sins and weaknesses of human nature, and of their remedies, and illustrating their observations by narratives, brief or elaborate,
from Holy Writ, sacred legend, ancient history, and romantic story. Thus Gower's book, as he says at its close,
stands "between earnest and game," and might be fairly
described as a *Romaunt of the Rose*, without either the
descriptive grace of Guillaume de Lorris, or the wicked
wit of Jean de Meung, but full of learning and matter, and
written by an author certainly not devoid of the art of telling stories. The mind of this author was thoroughly didactic in its bent; for the beauty of nature he has no real
feeling; and though his poem, like so many of Chaucer's,
begins in the month of May, he is (unnecessarily) careful
to tell us that his object in going forth was not to "sing
with the birds." He could not, like Chaucer, transfuse
old things into new, but there is enough in his character
as a poet to explain the friendship between the pair, of
which we hear at the very time when Gower was probably
preparing his *Confessio Amantis* for publication.

They are said afterwards to have become enemies; but
in the absence of any real evidence to that effect, we cannot believe Chaucer to have been likely to quarrel with
one whom he had certainly both trusted and admired.
Nor had literary life in England already advanced to a
stage of development of which, as in the Elizabethan and
Augustan ages, literary jealousy was an indispensable ac-

companiment. Chaucer is supposed to have attacked
Gower in a passage of the *Canterbury Tales*, where he incidentally declares his dislike (in itself extremely commend-
able) of a particular kind of sensational stories, instancing
the subject of one of the numerous tales in the *Confessio
Amantis*. There is, however, no reason whatever for supposing Chaucer to have here intended a reflection on his
brother poet, more especially as the *Man of Law*, after ut-
tering the censure, relates, though probably not from Gower, a story on a subject of a different kind likewise treated
by him. It is scarcely more suspicious that when Gower,
in a second edition of his chief work, dedicated in 1393
to Henry, Earl of Derby (afterwards Henry IV.), judiciously omitted the exordium and altered the close of the first
edition—both of which were complimentary to Richard II.
—he left out, together with its surrounding context, a passage conveying a friendly challenge to Chaucer as a "disciple and poet of the God of Love."

In any case there could have been no political difference
between them, for Chaucer was at all times in favour with
the House of Lancaster, towards whose future head Gower
so early contrived to assume a correct attitude. To him
—a man of substance, with landed property in three
counties—the rays of immediate court-favour were probably of less importance than to Chaucer; but it is not
necessity only which makes courtiers of so many of us:
some are born to the vocation, and Gower strikes one as
naturally more prudent and cautious—in short, more of
a politic personage—than Chaucer. He survived him
eight years—a blind invalid, in whose mind at least we
may hope nothing dimmed or blurred the recollection of
a friend to whom he owes much of his fame.

In a still nearer relationship—on which the works of

Chaucer that may certainly or probably be assigned to this period throw some light—it seems impossible to describe him as having been fortunate.   Whatever may have been the date and circumstances of his marriage, it seems, at all events in its later years, not to have been a happy one. The allusions to Chaucer's personal experience of married life in both *Troilus and Cressid* and the *House of Fame* are not of a kind to be entirely explicable by that tendency to make a mock of women and of marriage, which has frequently been characteristic of satirists, and which was specially popular in an age cherishing the wit of Jean de Meung, and complacently corroborating its theories from naughty Latin fables, French *fabliaux*, and Italian *novelle*. Both in *Troilus and Cressid* and in the *House of Fame* the poet's tone, when he refers to himself, is generally dolorous; but while both poems contain unmistakeable references to the joylessness of his own married life, in the latter he speaks of himself as "suffering debonairly"—or, as we should say, putting a good face upon—a state "desperate of all bliss."   And it is a melancholy though half sarcastic glimpse into his domestic privacy which he incidentally, and it must be allowed rather unnecessarily, gives in the following passage of the same poem :—

> "'Awake!' to me he said,
> In voice and tone the very same
> *That useth one whom I could name ;*
> And with that voice, sooth to say(n)
> My mind returned to me again ;
> For it was goodly said to me ;
> So was it never wont to be."

In other words, the kindness of the voice reassured him that it was *not* the same as that which he was wont to hear close to his pillow ! Again, the entire tone of the

Prologue to the *Legend of Good Women* is not that of a happy lover; although it would be pleasant enough, considering that the lady who imposes on the poet the penalty of celebrating *good* women is Alcestis, the type of faithful wifehood, to interpret the poem as not only an *amende honorable* to the female sex in general, but a token of reconciliation to the poet's wife in particular. Even in the joyous *Assembly of Fowls*, a marriage-poem, the same discord already makes itself heard; for it cannot be without meaning that in his dream the poet is told by "African"—

> ". . . Thou of love hast lost thy taste, I guess,
> As sick men have of sweet and bitterness;"

and that he confesses for himself that, though he has read much of love, he knows not of it by experience. While, however, we reluctantly accept the conclusion that Chaucer was unhappy as a husband, we must at the same time decline, because the husband was a poet, and one of the most genial of poets, to cast all the blame upon the wife, and to write her down a shrew. It is unfortunate, no doubt, but it is likewise inevitable, that at so great a distance of time the rights and wrongs of a conjugal disagreement or estrangement cannot with safety be adjusted. Yet again, because we refuse to blame Philippa, we are not obliged to blame Chaucer. At the same time, it must not be concealed that his name occurs in the year 1380 in connexion with a legal process, of which the most obvious, though not the only possible, explanation is that he had been guilty of a grave infidelity towards his wife. Such discoveries as this last we might be excused for wishing unmade.

Considerable uncertainty remains with regard to the dates of the poems belonging to this seemingly, in all re-

spects but one, fortunate period of Chaucer's life. Of one
of these works, however, which has had the curious fate
to be dated and re-dated by a succession of happy conjectures, the last and happiest of all may be held to have definitively fixed the occasion. This is the charming poem
called the *Assembly of Fowls*, or *Parliament of Birds*—a
production which seems so English, so fresh from nature's
own inspiration, so instinct with the gaiety of Chaucer's
own heart, that one is apt to overlook in it the undeniable
vestiges of foreign influences, both French and Italian.
At its close the poet confesses that he is always reading,
and therefore hopes that he may at last read something
"so to fare the better." But with all this evidence of
study the *Assembly of Fowls* is chiefly interesting as showing how Chaucer had now begun to select as well as to
assimilate his loans; how, while he was still moving along
well-known tracks, his eyes were joyously glancing to the
right and the left; and how the source of most of his
imagery, at all events, he already found in the merry England around him, even as he had chosen for his subject
one of real national interest.

Anne of Bohemia, daughter of the great Emperor
Charles IV., and sister of King Wenceslas, had been suc-
cessively betrothed to a Bavarian prince and to a Margrave
of Meissen, before—after negotiations which, according to
Froissart, lasted a year—her hand was given to the young
King Richard II. of England. This sufficiently explains
the general scope of the *Assembly of Fowls*, an allegorical
poem written on or about St. Valentine's Day, 1381—
eleven months, or nearly a year, after which date the marriage took place. On the morning sacred to lovers, the
poet (in a dream, of course, and this time conducted by
the arch-dreamer Scipio in person) enters a garden con-

taining in it the temple of the God of Love, and filled with
inhabitants mythological and allegorical.   Here he sees
the noble goddess Nature, seated upon a hill of flowers, and
around her " all the fowls that be," assembled as by time-
honoured custom on St. Valentine's Day, "when every
fowl comes there to choose her mate."   Their huge noise
and hubbub is reduced to order by Nature, who assigns to
each fowl its proper place—the birds of prey highest ; then
those that eat according to natural inclination—

> "Worm or thing of which I tell no tale ;"

then those that live by seed ; and the various members of
the several classes are indicated with amusing vivacity and
point, from the royal eagle "that with his sharp look
pierceth the sun," and "other eagles of a lower kind"
downwards.   We can only find room for a portion of the
company :—

> "The sparrow, Venus' son ; the nightingale
> That clepeth forth the freshë leavës new ;
> The swallow, murd'rer of the beës small,
> That honey make of flowers fresh of hue ;
> The wedded turtle, with his heartë true ;
> The peacock, with his angels' feathers bright,
> The pheasant, scorner of the cock by night.

> "The waker goose, the cuckoo, ever unkind ;
> The popinjay, full of delícacy ;
> The drake, destroyer of his ownë kind ;
> The stork, avenger of adultery ;
> The cormorant, hot and full of gluttony ;
> The crows and ravens with their voice of care ;
> And the throstle old, and the frostý fieldfáre."

Naturalists must be left to explain some of these epithets
and designations, not all of which rest on allusions as easily

understood as that recalling the goose's exploit on the
Capitol; but the vivacity of the whole description speaks
for itself. One is reminded of Aristophanes' feathered
chorus; but birds are naturally the delight of poets, and
were befriended by Dante himself.

Hereupon the action of the poem opens. A female
eagle is wooed by three suitors — all eagles; but among
them the first, or royal eagle, discourses in the manner
most likely to conciliate favour. Before the answer is
given, a pause furnishes an opportunity to the other fowls
for delighting in the sound of their own voices, Dame
Nature proposing that each class of birds shall, through
the beak of its representative "agitator," express its opinion on the problem before the assembly. There is much
humour in the readiness of the goose to rush in with a
ready-made resolution, and in the smart reproof adminis-
tered by the sparrow-hawk amidst the uproar of "the gentle fowls all." At last Nature silences the tumult, and the
lady-eagle delivers her answer, to the effect that she cannot
make up her mind for a year to come; but inasmuch as
Nature has advised her to choose the royal eagle, his is
clearly the most favourable prospect. Whereupon, after
certain fowls had sung a roundel, "as was always the
usance," the assembly, like some human Parliaments,
breaks up with shouting;[1] and the dreamer awakes to re-
sume his reading.

Very possibly the *Assembly of Fowls* was at no great
interval of time either followed or preceded by two poems
of far inferior interest—the *Complaint of Mars* (apparently afterwards amalgamated with that of *Venus*), which is

---

[1] "Than all the birdis song with sic a schout
   That I annone awoik quhair that I lay."
                    DUNBAR, *The Thrissill and the Rois.*

supposed to be sung by a bird on St. Valentine's morning, and the fragment *Of Queen Anelida and false Arcite*.
There are, however, reasons which make a less early date
probable in the case of the latter production, the history
of the origin and purpose of which can hardly be said as
yet to be .removed out of the region of mere speculation.
In any case, neither of these poems can be looked upon as
preparations, on Chaucer's part, for the longer work on
which he was to expend so much labour; but in a sense
this description would apply to the translation which,
probably before he wrote *Troilus and Cressid*, certainly
before he wrote the Prologue to the *Legend of Good
Women*, he made of the famous Latin work of Boëthius,
"the just man in prison," on the *Consolation of Philosophy*. This book was, and very justly so, one of the favourite manuals of the Middle Ages, and a treasure-house
of religious wisdom to centuries of English writers.
"Boice of Consolacioun" is cited in the *Romaunt of the
Rose;* and the list of passages imitated by Chaucer from
the martyr of Catholic orthodoxy and Roman freedom
of speech is exceedingly long. Among them are the ever-
recurring diatribe against the fickleness of fortune, and
(through the medium of Dante) the reflection on the distinction between gentle birth and a gentle life. Chaucer's
translation was not made at second-hand; if not always
easy, it is conscientious, and interpolated with numerous
glosses and explanations thought necessary by the translator. The metre of *The Former Life* he at one time or
another turned into verse of his own.

Perhaps the most interesting of the quotations made in
Chaucer's poems from Boëthius occurs in his *Troilus and
Cressid*, one of the many mediæval versions of an episode
engrafted by the lively fancy of an Anglo-Norman *trouvère*

5

upon the deathless, and in its literary variations incomparably luxuriant, growth of the story of Troy. On Benoît de Sainte-Maure's poem Guido de Colonna founded his Latin-prose romance; and this again, after being reproduced in languages and by writers almost innumerable, served Boccaccio as the foundation of his poem *Filostrato* —*i. e.*, the victim of love. All these works, together with Chaucer's *Troilus and Cressid*, with Lydgate's *Troy-Book*, with Henryson's *Testament of Cressid* (and in a sense even with Shakspeare's drama on the theme of Chaucer's poem), may be said to belong to the second cycle of modern versions of the tale of Troy divine. Already their earlier predecessors had gone far astray from Homer, of whom they only knew by hearsay, relying for their facts on late Latin epitomes, which freely mutilated and perverted the Homeric narrative in favour of the Trojans—the supposed ancestors of half the nations of Europe. Accordingly, Chaucer, in a well-known passage in his *House of Fame*, regrets, with sublime coolness, how " one said that Homer " wrote " lies,"

> " Feigning in his poetries
> And was to Greekës favouráble.
> Therefore held he it but fable."

But the courtly poets of the romantic age of literature went a step further, and added a mediæval colouring all their own. One converts the Sibyl into a nun, and makes her admonish Æneas to tell his beads. Another — it is Chaucer's successor Lydgate—introduces Priam's sons exercising their bodies in tournaments and their minds in the glorious play of chess, and causes the memory of Hector to be consecrated by the foundation of a chantry of priests who are to pray for the repose of his soul. A third final-

ly condemns the erring Cressid to be stricken with leprosy, and to wander about with cup and clapper, like the unhappy lepers in the great cities of the Middle Ages. Everything, in short, is transfused by the spirit of the adapt-
ers' own times; and so far are these writers from any weak-
ly sense of anachronism in describing Troy as if it were
a moated and turreted city of the later Middle Ages, that
they are only careful now and then to protest their own
truthfulness when anything in their narrative seems *unlike*
the days in which they write.

But Chaucer, though his poem is, to start with, only an
English reproduction of an Italian version of a Latin translation of a French poem, and though in most respects it
shares the characteristic features of the body of poetic fiction to which it belongs, is far from being a mere translator. Apart from several remarkable reminiscences introduced by Chaucer from Dante, as well as from the irrepressible *Romaunt of the Rose*, he has changed his original in points which are not mere matters of detail or questions of convenience. In accordance with the essentially
dramatic bent of his own genius, some of these changes
have reference to the aspect of the characters and the conduct of the plot, as well as to the whole spirit of the conception of the poem. Cressid (who, by the way, is a widow at the outset—whether she had children or not Chaucer nowhere found stated, and therefore leaves undecided)
may at first sight strike the reader as a less consistent
character in Chaucer than in Boccaccio. But there is true
art in the way in which, in the English poem, our sympathy is first aroused for the heroine, whom, in the end, we
cannot but condemn. In Boccaccio, Cressid is fair and
false—one of those fickle creatures with whom Italian literature, and Boccaccio in particular, so largely deal, and

whose presentment merely repeats to us the old cynical
half-truth as to woman's weakness. The English poet,
though he does not pretend that his heroine was "religious" (*i.e.*, a nun to whom earthly love is a sin), endears
her to us from the first; so much that "O the pity of it"
seems the hardest verdict we can ultimately pass upon her
conduct. How, then, is the catastrophe of the action, the
falling away of Cressid from her truth to Troilus, poetical-
ly explained? By an appeal—pedantically put, perhaps,
and as it were dragged in violently by means of a truncated
quotation from Boëthius—to the fundamental difficulty
concerning the relations between poor human life and the
government of the world. This, it must be conceded, is
a considerably deeper problem than the nature of woman.
Troilus and Cressid, the hero sinned against and the sinning
heroine, are the *victims of Fate.* Who shall cast a stone
against those who are, but like the rest of us, predestined
to their deeds and to their doom; since the co-existence
of free-will with predestination does not admit of proof?
This solution of the conflict may be morally as well as
theologically unsound; it certainly is æsthetically faulty;
but it is the reverse of frivolous or commonplace.

Or let us turn from Cressid, "matchless in beauty,"
and warm with sweet life, but not ignoble even in the season of her weakness, to another personage of the poem.
In itself the character of Pandarus is one of the most re-
volting which imagination can devise; so much so that the
name has become proverbial for the most despicable of
human types. With Boccaccio Pandarus is Cressid's cous-
in and Troilus' youthful friend, and there is no intention
of making him more offensive than are half the confidants
of amorous heroes. But Chaucer sees his dramatic opportunity; and without painting black in black and creat-

ing a monster of vice, he invents a good-natured and lo-
quacious elderly go-between, full of proverbial philosophy
and invaluable experience—a genuine light comedy character for all times. How admirably this Pandarus prac-
tises as well as preaches his art; using the hospitable
Deiphobus and the queenly Helen as unconscious instru-
ments in his intrigue for bringing the lovers together:—

> "She came to dinner in her plain intent;
> But God and Pandar wist what all this meant."

Lastly, considering the extreme length of Chaucer's
poem, and the very simple plot of the story which it tells,
one cannot fail to admire the skill with which the conduct
of its action is managed. In Boccaccio the earlier part of
the story is treated with brevity, while the conclusion, after the catastrophe has occurred and the main interest has
passed, is long drawn out. Chaucer dwells at great length
upon the earlier and pleasing portion of the tale, more
especially on the falling in love of Cressid, which is worked out with admirable naturalness. But he comparatively
hastens over its pitiable end — the fifth and last book of
his poem corresponding to not less than four cantos of
the *Filostrato*. In Chaucer's hands, therefore, the story is
a real love-story; and the more that we are led to rejoice
with the lovers in their bliss, the more our compassion is
excited by the lamentable end of so much happiness; and
we feel at one with the poet, who, after lingering over the
happiness of which he has in the end to narrate the fall, as
it were, unwillingly proceeds to accomplish his task, and
bids his readers be wroth with the destiny of his heroine
rather than with himself. His own heart, he says, bleeds
and his pen quakes to write what must be written of the
falsehood of Cressid, which was her doom.

Chaucer's nature, however tried, was unmistakeably one gifted with the blessed power of easy self-recovery. Though it was in a melancholy vein that he had begun to write *Troilus and Cressid*, he had found opportunities enough in the course of the poem for giving expression to the fresh vivacity and playful humour which are justly reckoned among his chief characteristics. And thus, towards its close, we are not surprised to find him apparently looking forward to a sustained effort of a kind more congenial to himself. He sends forth his "little book, his little tragedy," with the prayer that, before he dies, God, his Maker, may send him might to "make some comedy." If the poem called the *House of Fame* followed upon *Troilus and Cressid* (the order of succession may, however, have been the reverse), then, although the poet's own mood had little altered, yet he had resolved upon essaying a direction which he rightly felt to be suitable to his genius.

The *House of Fame* has not been distinctly traced to any one foreign source; but the influence of both Petrarch and Dante, as well as that of classical authors, are clearly to be traced in the poem. And yet this work, Chaucer's most ambitious attempt in poetical allegory, may be described not only as in the main due to an original conception, but as representing the results of the writer's personal experience. All things considered, it is the production of a man of wonderful reading, and shows that Chaucer's was a mind interested in the widest variety of subjects, which drew no invidious distinctions, such as we moderns are prone to insist upon, between Arts and Science, but (notwithstanding an occasional deprecatory modesty) eagerly sought to familiarise itself with the achievements of both. In a passage concerning the men of letters who had found a place in the *House of Fame*, he displays not only an acquaintance with the names of several ancient classics, but also a keen appreciation—now and then, perhaps, due to instinct—of their several characteristics. Elsewhere he shows his interest in scientific inquiry by references to such matters as the theory of sound and the Arabic system of numeration; while the Mentor of the poem, the Eagle, openly boasts his powers of clear scientific demonstration, in averring that he can speak "lewdly" (*i. e.*, popularly) "to a lewd man." The poem opens with a very fresh and lively discussion of the question of dreams in general—a semi-scientific subject which much occupied Chaucer, and upon which even Pandarus and the wedded couple of the *Nun's Priest's Tale* expend their philosophy.

Thus, besides giving evidence of considerable information and study, the *House of Fame* shows Chaucer to have been gifted with much natural humour. Among its happy touches are the various rewards bestowed by Fame upon the claimants for her favour, including the ready grant of evil fame to those who desire it (a bad name, to speak colloquially, is to be had for the asking); and the wonderful paucity of those who wish their good works to remain in obscurity and to be their own reward, but then Chaucer was writing in the Middle Ages. And as, pointing in a direction which the author of the poem was subsequently to follow out, we may also specially notice the company thronging the House of Rumour: shipmen and pilgrims, the two most numerous kinds of travellers in Chaucer's age, fresh from seaport and sepulchre, with scrips brimful of unauthenticated intelligence. In short, this poem offers in its details much that is characteristic of its author's genius; while, as a whole, its abrupt termina-

tion notwithstanding, it leaves the impression of completeness.   The allegory, simple and clear in construction, ful-
fils the purpose for which it was devised; the conceptions
upon which it is based are neither idle, like many of those
in Chaucer's previous allegories, nor are they so artificial
and far-fetched as to fatigue instead of stimulating the
mind.   Pope, who reproduced parts of the *House of Fame*
in a loose paraphrase, in attempting to improve the construction of Chaucer's work, only mutilated it.   As it
stands, it is clear and digestible; and how many allegories,
one may take leave to ask, in our own allegory-loving literature or in any other, merit the same commendation?   For
the rest, Pope's own immortal *Dunciad*, though doubtless
more immediately suggested by a personal satire of Dryden's, is in one sense a kind of travesty of the *House of
Fame*—a *House of Infamy*.

In the theme of this poem there was undoubtedly something that could hardly fail to humour the half-melancholy mood in which it was manifestly written.   Are not,
the poet could not but ask himself, all things vanity—" as
men say, what may ever last?"   Yet the subject brought
its consolation likewise.   Patient labour, such as this poem
attests, is the surest road to that enduring fame, which is
" conserved with the shade;" and awaking from his vision, Chaucer takes leave of the reader with a resolution
already habitual to him—to read more and more, instead
of resting satisfied with the knowledge he has already acquired.   And in the last of the longer poems which seem
assignable to this period of his life, he proves that one
Latin poet at least—Venus' clerk, whom in the *House of
Fame* he beheld standing on a pillar of her own Cyprian
metal—had been read as well as celebrated by him.

Of this poem, the fragmentary *Legend of Good Women*,

the *Prologue* possesses a peculiar biographical as well as literary interest. In his personal feelings on the subject of love and marriage, Chaucer had, when he wrote this *Prologue*, evidently almost passed even beyond the sarcastic stage. And as a poet he was now clearly conscious of being no longer a beginner, no longer a learner only, but one whom his age knew, and in whom it took a critical interest. The list including most of his undoubted works, which he here recites, shows of itself that those already spoken of in the foregoing pages were by this time known to the world, together with two of the *Canterbury Tales*, which had either been put forth independently, or (as seems much less probable) had formed the first instalment of his great work. A further proof of the relatively late date of this *Prologue* occurs in the contingent offer which it makes of the poem to " the Queen," who can be no other than Richard II.'s young consort Anne. At the very outset we find Chaucer, as it were, reviewing his own literary position—and doing so in the spirit of an author who knows very well what is said against him, who knows very well what there is in what is said against him, and who yet is full of that true self-consciousness which holds to its course — not recklessly and ruthlessly, not with a contempt for the feelings and judgments of his fellow-creatures, but with a serene trust in the justification ensured to every honest endeavour. The principal theme of his poems had hitherto been the passion of love, and woman, who is the object of the love of man. Had he not, the superfine critics of his day may have asked—steeped as they were in the artificiality and florid extravagance of chivalry in the days of its decline, and habituated to mistranslating earthly passion into the phraseology of religious devotion — had he not debased

5*

the passion of love, and defamed its object? Had he not
begun by translating the wicked satire of Jean de Meung,
"a heresy against the law" of Love? and had he not, by
cynically painting in his Cressid a picture of woman's
perfidy, encouraged men to be less faithful to women

> "That be as true as ever was any steel?"

In Chaucer's way of meeting this charge, which he em-
phasises by putting it in the mouth of the God of Love
himself, it is, to be sure, difficult to recognise any very
deeply penitent spirit. He mildly wards off the reproach,
sheltering himself behind his defender, the "lady in green,"
who afterwards proves to be herself that type of womanly
and wifely fidelity unto death, the true and brave Alcestis.
And even in the body of the poem one is struck by a certain perfunctoriness, not to say flippancy, in the way in
which its moral is reproduced. The wrathful invective
against the various classical followers of Lamech, the
maker of tents,[1] wears no aspect of deep moral indignation; and it is not precisely the voice of a repentant sin-

---

[1] Lamech, Chaucer tells us in *Queen Annelida and the false Arcite*,
was the
> "First father that began
> The love of two, and was in bigamy."

This poem seems designed to illustrate much the same moral as
that enforced by the *Legend of Good Women*—a moral which, by-the-
bye, is already foreshadowed towards the close of *Troilus and Cressid*, where Chaucer speaks of

> "Women that betrayèd be
> Through falsë folk (God give them sorrow, amen!),
> That with their greatë wit and subtlety
> Betray you; and 'tis this that moveth me
> To speak; and, in effect, you all I pray:
> Beware of men, and hearken what I say."

ner which concludes the pathetic story of the betrayal of
Phillis with the adjuration to ladies in general :—

> " Beware ye women of your subtle foe,
>   Since yet this day men may example see ;
>   And as in love trust ye no man but me."

At the same time the poet lends an attentive ear, as genius
can always afford to do, to a criticism of his shortcomings, and readily accepts the sentence pronounced by Alcestis, that he shall write a legend of *good* women, both
maidens and also wives, that were

> " True in loving all their lives."

And thus, with the courage of a good or, at all events,
easy conscience, he sets about his task which unfortunately
—it is conjectured by reason of domestic calamities, probably including the death of his wife—remained, or at least
has come down to us unfinished.   We have only nine of
the nineteen stories which he appears to have intended to
present (though, indeed, a manuscript of Henry IV.'s reign
quotes Chaucer's book of " xxv good women ").   It is by
no means necessary to suppose that all these nine stories
were written continuously ; maybe, too, Chaucer, with all
his virtuous intentions, grew tired of his rather monotonous scheme at a time when he was beginning to busy
himself with stories meant to be fitted into the more liberal framework of the *Canterbury Tales*.   All these illustrations of female constancy are of classical origin, as
Chaucer is glad to make known ; and most of them are
taken from Ovid.   But though the thread of the English
poet's narratives is supplied by such established favourites
as the stories of Cleopatra, the Martyr Queen of Egypt;
of Thisbe of Babylon, the Martyr; and of Dido, to whom

"Æneas was forsworn," yet he by no means slavishly adheres to his authorities, but alters or omits in accordance with the design of his book. Thus, for instance, we read of Medea's desertion by Jason, but hear nothing of her as the murderess of her children; while, on the other hand, the tragedy of Dido is enhanced by pathetic additions not to be found in Virgil. Modern taste may dislike the way in which this poem mixes up the terms and ideas of Christian martyrology with classical myths, and as "the Legend of the Saints of Cupid" assumes the character of a kind of calendar of women canonised by reason of their faithfulness to earthly love. But obviously this is a method of treatment belonging to an age, not to a single poem or poet. Chaucer's artistic judgment in the selection and arrangement of his themes, the wonderful vivacity and true pathos with which he turns upon Tarquin or Jason as if they had personally offended him, and his genuine flow of feeling not only *for* but *with* his unhappy heroines, add a new charm to the old familiar faces. Proof is thus furnished, if any proof were needed, that no story interesting in itself is too old to admit of being told again by a poet; in Chaucer's version Ovid loses something in polish, but nothing in pathos; and the breezy freshness of nature seems to be blowing through tales which became the delight of a nation's, as they have been that of many a man's, youth.

A single passage must suffice to illustrate the style of the *Legend of Good Women;* and it shall be the lament 'of Ariadne, the concluding passage of the story which is the typical tale of desertion, though not, as it remains in Chaucer, of desertion unconsoled. It will be seen how far the English poet's vivacity is from being extinguished by the pathos of the situation described by him.

"Right in the dawëning awaketh she,
And gropeth in the bed, and found right nought.
'Alas,' quoth she, 'that ever I was wrought!
I am betrayèd!' and her hair she rent,
And to the strandë barefoot fast she went,
And criedë: 'Theseus, mine heartë sweet!
Where be ye, that I may not with you meet?
And mightë thus by beastës been y-slain!'
The hollow rockës answered her again.
No man she sawë; and yet shone the moon,
And high upon a rock she wentë soon,
And saw his bargë sailing in the sea.
Cold waxed her heart, and right thus saidë she:
    'Meeker than ye I find the beastës wild!'
(Hath he not sin that he her thus beguiled?)
She cried, 'O turn again for ruth and sin,
Thy bargë hath not all thy meinie in.'
Her kerchief on a polë stickèd she,
Askancë, that he should it well y-see,
And should remember that she was behind,
And turn again, and on the strand her find.
But all for naught; his way he is y-gone,
And down she fell aswoonë on a stone;
And up she rose, and kissed, in all her care,
The steppës of his feet remaining there;
And then unto her bed she speaketh so:
    'Thou bed,' quoth she, 'that hast receivèd two,
Thou shalt answér for two, and not for one;
Where is the greater part away y-gone?
Alas, what shall I wretched wight become?
For though so be no help shall hither come,
Home to my country dare I not for dread,
I can myselfë in this case not rede.'
Why should I tell more of her cómplaining?
It is so long it were a heavy thing.
In her Epistle Naso telleth all.
But shortly to the endë tell I shall.
The goddës have her holpen for pity,
And in the sign of Taurus men may see

> The stonës of her crown all shining clear.
> I will no further speak of this mattér.
> But thus these falsë lovers can beguile
> Their truë love; the devil quite him his while!"

Manifestly, then, in this period of his life—if a chronology which is in a great measure conjectural may be accepted—Chaucer had been a busy worker, and his pen had
covered many a page with the results of his rapid productivity.   Perhaps his *Words unto his own Scrivener*, which
we may fairly date about this time, were rather too hard
on "Adam."   Authors *are* often hard on persons who
have to read their handiwork professionally; but, in the
interest of posterity, poets may be permitted an execration
or two against whosoever changes their words as well as
against whosoever moves their bones:—

> "Adam Scrivener, if ever it thee befall
> *Boece* or *Troilus* to write anew,
> Under thy long locks may'st thou have the scall,
> If thou my writing copy not more true!
> So oft a day I must thy work renew,
> It to correct and eke to rub and scrape;
> And all is through thy negligence and rape."

How far the manuscript of the *Canterbury Tales* had
already progressed is uncertain; the *Prologue* to the
Legend of Good Women mentions the *Love of Palamon
and Arcite* — an earlier version of the *Knight's Tale*, if
not identical with it—and a *Life of Saint Cecilia* which
is preserved, apparently without alteration, in the *Second
Nun's Tale*.   Possibly other stories had been already added to these, and the *Prologue* written—but this is more
than can be asserted with safety.   Who shall say whether, if the stream of prosperity had continued to flow, on
which the bark of Chaucer's fortunes had for some years

been borne along, he might not have found leisure and impulse sufficient for completing his masterpiece, or, at all
events, for advancing it near to completion? That his powers declined with his years, is a conjecture which it would
be difficult to support by satisfactory evidence; though it
seems natural enough to assume that he wrote the best of
his *Canterbury Tales* in his best days. Troubled times
we know to have been in store for him. The reverse in
his fortunes may perhaps fail to call forth in us the sympathy which we feel for Milton in his old age doing battle against a Philistine reaction, or for Spenser, over-
whelmed with calamities at the end of a life full of bit-
ter disappointment. But at least we may look upon
it with the respectful pity which we entertain for Ben
Jonson groaning in the midst of his literary honours
under that *dura rerum necessitas*, which is rarely more
a matter of indifference to poets than it is to other
men.

In 1386, as already noted, Chaucer, while continuing to
hold both his offices at the Customs, had taken his seat in
Parliament as one of the knights of the shire of Kent. He
had attained to this honour during the absence in Spain
of his patron, the Duke of Lancaster, though probably he
had been elected in the interest of that prince. But
John of Gaunt's influence was inevitably reduced to nothing during his absence, and no doubt King Richard now
hoped to be a free agent. But he very speedily found
that the hand of his younger uncle, Thomas, Duke of
Gloucester, was heavier upon him than that of the elder.
The Parliament of which Chaucer was a member was the
assembly which boldly confronted the autocratical tendencies of Richard II., and after overthrowing the Chan-
cellor, Michael de la Pole, Earl of Suffolk, forced upon the

King a Council controlling the administration of affairs.
Concerning the acts of this Council, of which Gloucester
was the leading member, little or nothing is known, except
that in financial matters it attempted, after the manner
of new brooms, to sweep clean. Soon the attention of
Gloucester and his following was occupied by subjects
more absorbing than a branch of reform fated to be treated
fitfully. In this instance the new administration had as
usual demanded its victims—and among their number was
Chaucer; for it can hardly be a mere coincidence that by
the beginning of December in this year, 1386, Chaucer had
lost one, and by the middle of the same month the other,
of his comptrollerships. At the same time, it would be
presumptuously unfair to conclude that misconduct of any
kind on his part had been the reason of his removal. The
explanation usually given is that he fell as an adherent of
John of Gaunt: perhaps a safer way of putting the matter
would be to say that John of Gaunt was no longer in England to protect him. Inasmuch as even reforming Gov-
ernments are occasionally as anxious about men as they
are about measures, Chaucer's posts may have been wanted
for nominees of the Duke of Gloucester and his Council
—such as it is probably no injustice to Masters Adam
Yerdely and Henry Gisors (who respectively succeeded
Chaucer in his two offices) to suppose them to have been.
Moreover, it is just possible that Chaucer was the reverse
of a *persona grata* to Gloucester's faction on account of the
Comptroller's previous official connexion with Sir Nicholas
Brembre, who, besides being hated in the city, had been
accused of seeking to compass the deaths of the Duke and
of some of his adherents. In any case, it is noticeable
that four months *before* the return to England of the Duke
of Lancaster—*i. e.*, in July, 1389—Chaucer was appointed

Clerk of the King's Works at Westminster, the Tower, and a large number of other royal manors or tenements, including (from 1390, at all events) St. George's Chapel, Windsor. In this office he was not ill-paid, receiving two shillings a day in money, and very possibly perquisites in addition, besides being allowed to appoint a deputy. Inasmuch as, in the summer of the year 1389, King Richard had assumed the reins of government in person, while the ascendency of Gloucester was drawing to a close, we may conclude the King to have been personally desirous to provide for a faithful and attached servant of his house, for whom he had had reason to feel a personal liking. It would be specially pleasing, were we able to connect with Chaucer's restoration to official employment the high-minded Queen Anne, whose impending betrothal he had probably celebrated in one poem, and whose patronage he had claimed for another.

The Clerkship of the King's Works, to which Chaucer was appointed, seems to have been but a temporary office; or at all events he only held it for rather less than two years, during part of which he performed its duties by deputy. Already, however, before his appointment to this post, he had certainly become involved in difficulties; for in May, 1388, we find his pensions, at his own request, assigned to another person (John Scalby)—a statement implying that he had raised money on them which he could only pay by making over the pensions themselves. Very possibly, too, he had, before his dismissal from his comptrollerships, been subjected to an enquiry which, if it did not touch his honour, at all events gave rise to very natural apprehensions on the part of himself and his friends. There is, accordingly, much probability in the conjecture which ascribes to this season of peril and pressure the

composition of the following justly famous stanzas, entitled
Good Counsel of Chaucer :—

> "Flee from the press, and dwell with soothfastness;
>   Sufficë thee thy good, though it be small;
> For hoard hath hate, and climbing tickleness:
>   Press hath envȳ, and wealth is blinded all.
> Savour no more than thee behovë shall;
>   Do well thyself that other folk canst rede;
>   And truth thee shall deliver, it is no dread.
>
> "Painë thee not each crooked to redress
>   In trust of her[1] that turneth as a ball.
> Greatë rest stands in little business.
>   Beware also to spurn against a nail.
> Strive not as doth a pitcher with a wall.
>   Deemë thyself that deemest others' deed;
>   And truth thee shall deliver, it is no dread.
>
> "That thee is sent receive in buxomness;
>   The wrestling of this world asketh a fall.
> Here is no home, here is but wilderness.
>   Forth, pilgrimë! forth, beast, out of thy stall!
> Look up on high, and thankë God of all.
>   Waivë thy lust, and let thy ghost thee lead,
>   And truth shall thee deliver, it is no dread."

Misfortunes, it is said, never come alone; and whatever
view may be taken as to the nature of the relations between Chaucer and his wife, her death cannot have left
him untouched. From the absence of any record as to
the payment of her pension after June, 1387, this event
is presumed to have taken place in the latter half of that
year. More than this cannot safely be conjectured; but
it remains *possible* that the *Legend of Good Women* and
its *Prologue* formed a peace-offering to one whom Chaucer may have loved again after he had lost her, though

---

[1] Fortune.

without thinking of her as of his "late departed saint."
Philippa Chaucer had left behind her a son of the name
of Lewis; and it is pleasing to find the widower in the
year 1391 (the year in which he lost his Clerkship of the
Works) attending to the boy's education, and supplying
him with the intellectual "bread and milk" suitable for
his tender age in the shape of a popular treatise on a subject which has at all times excited the intelligent curiosity
of the young. The treatise *On the Astrolabe*, after describing the instrument itself, and showing how to work
it, proceeded, or was intended to proceed, to fulfil the purposes of a general astronomical manual; but, like other
and more important works of its author, it has come down
to us in an uncompleted, or at all events incomplete, condition. What there is of it was, as a matter of course, not
original — popular scientific books rarely are. The little
treatise, however, possesses a double interest for the student
of Chaucer. In the first place, it shows explicitly, what
several passages imply, that while he was to a certain extent
fond of astronomical study (as to his capacity for which
he clearly does injustice to himself in the *House of Fame*),
his good sense and his piety alike revolted against extravagant astrological speculations. He certainly does not
wish to go as far as the honest carpenter in the *Miller's
Tale*, who glories in his incredulity of aught besides his
credo, and who yet is afterwards befooled by the very im-
postor of whose astrological pursuits he had reprehended
the impiety. "Men," he says, "should know nothing of
that which is private to God. Yea, blessed be alway a
simple man who knows nothing but only his belief." In
his little work *On the Astrolabe* Chaucer speaks with calm
reasonableness of superstitions in which his spirit has no
faith, and pleads guilty to ignorance of the useless knowl-

edge with which they are surrounded. But the other, and
perhaps the chief value, to us of this treatise lies in the
fact that of Chaucer in an intimate personal relation it
contains the only picture in which it is impossible to suspect any false or exaggerated colouring. For here we have
him writing to his "little Lewis" with fatherly satisfaction
in the ability displayed by the boy "to learn sciences
touching numbers and proportions," and telling how, after
making a present to the child of "a sufficient astrolabe as
for our own horizon, composed after the latitude of Oxford," he has further resolved to explain to him a certain
number of conclusions connected with the purposes of the
instrument. This he has made up his mind to do in a
forcible as well as simple way; for he has shrewdly di-
vined a secret, now and then overlooked by those who
condense sciences for babes, that children need to be taught
a few things not only clearly but fully—repetition being in
more senses than one "the mother of studies:"—

"Now will I pray meekly every discreet person that readeth or
heareth this little treatise, to hold my rude inditing excused, and my
superfluity of words, for two causes. The first cause is: that curious
inditing and hard sentences are full heavy at once for such a child
to learn. And the second cause is this: that truly it seems better
to me to write unto a child twice a good sentence than to forget it
once."

Unluckily we know nothing further of Lewis—not even
whether, as has been surmised, he died before he had been
able to turn to lucrative account his calculating powers,
after the fashion of his apocryphal brother Thomas or
otherwise.

Though by the latter part of the year 1391 Chaucer had
lost his Clerkship of the Works, certain payments (possibly
of arrears) seem afterwards to have been made to him in

connexion with the office. A very disagreeable incident
of his tenure of it had been a double robbery from his
person of official money, to the very serious extent of
twenty pounds. The perpetrators of the crime were a
notorious gang of highwaymen, by whom Chaucer was, in
September, 1390, apparently on the same day, beset both
at Westminster and near to "the foul Oak" at Hatcham,
in Surrey. A few months afterwards he was discharged
by writ from repayment of the loss to the Crown. His
experiences during the three years following are unknown;
but in 1394 (when things were fairly quiet in England)
he was granted an annual pension of twenty pounds by
the King. This pension, of which several subsequent
notices occur, seems at times to have been paid tardily or
in small instalments, and also to have been frequently anticipated by Chaucer in the shape of loans of small sums.
Further evidence of his straits is to be found in his having, in the year 1398, obtained letters of protection against
arrest, making him safe for two years. The grant of a tun
of wine in October of the same year is the last favour
known to have been extended to Chaucer by King Richard II. Probably no English sovereign has been more diversely estimated, both by his contemporaries and by posterity, than this ill-fated prince, in the records of whose
career many passages betokening high spirit strangely contrast with the impotence of its close. It will at least be
remembered in his favour that he was a patron of the
arts; and that after Froissart had been present at his
christening, he received, when on the threshold of manhood, the homage of Gower, and on the eve of his downfall showed most seasonable kindness to a poet far greater
than either of these. It seems scarcely justifiable to assign to any particular point of time the *Ballade sent to*

King Richard by Chaucer; but its manifest intention was to apprise the King of the poet's sympathy with his struggle against the opponents of the royal policy, which was a thoroughly autocratical one. Considering the nature of the relations between the pair, nothing could be more unlikely than that Chaucer should have taken upon himself to exhort his sovereign and patron to steadfastness of political conduct. And in truth, though the loyal tone of this address is (as already observed) unmistakeable enough, there is little difficulty in accounting for the mixture of commonplace reflexions and of admonitions to the King, to persist in a spirited domestic policy. He is to

> "Dread God, do law, love truth and worthiness,"

and wed his people — not himself — "again to steadfastness." However, even a quasi-political poem of this description, whatever element of implied flattery it may contain, offers pleasanter reading than those least attractive of all occasional poems, of which the burden is a cry for money. The *Envoy to Scogan* has been diversely dated and diversely interpreted. The reference in these lines to a deluge of pestilence clearly means, not a pestilence produced by heavy rains, but heavy rains which might be expected to produce a pestilence. The primary purpose of the epistle admits of no doubt, though it is only revealed in the postscript. After bantering his friend on account of his faint-heartedness in love—

> "Because thy lady saw not thy distress,
> Therefore thou gavest her up at Michaelmas—"

Chaucer ends by entreating him to further his claims upon the royal munificence. Of this friend, Henry Scogan, a tradition repeated by Ben Jonson averred that he was a

fine gentleman and Master of Arts of Henry IV.'s time,
who was regarded and rewarded for his Court "disguis-
ings" and "writings in ballad-royal." He is, therefore, appropriately apostrophised by Chaucer as kneeling

> ". . . At the streamës head
> Of grace, of all honoúr and worthiness,"

and reminded that his friend is at the other end of the
current. The weariness of tone, natural under the circumstances, obscures whatever humour the poem possesses.

Very possibly the lines to Scogan were written not before, but immediately after, the accession of Henry IV.
In that case they belong to about the same date as the
well-known and very plain-spoken *Complaint of Chaucer to
his Purse,* addressed by him to the new Sovereign without
loss of time, if not indeed, as it would be hardly unchari-
table to suppose, prepared beforehand. Even in this *Complaint* (the term was a technical one for an elegiac piece,
and was so used by Spenser) there is a certain frank ge-
niality of tone, the natural accompaniment of an easy
conscience, which goes some way to redeem the nature of
the subject. Still, the theme remains one which only an
exceptionally skilful treatment can make sufficiently pathetic or perfectly comic. The lines had the desired effect; for within four days after his accession — *i. e.,* on
October 3rd, 1399 — the "conqueror of Brut's Albion,"
otherwise King Henry IV., doubled Chaucer's pension of
twenty marks, so that, continuing as he did to enjoy the
annuity of twenty pounds granted him by King Richard,
he was now once more in comfortable circumstances. The
best proof of these lies in the fact that very speedily—
on Christmas Eve, 1399 — Chaucer, probably in a rather
sanguine mood, covenanted for the lease for fifty-three

years of a house in the garden of the chapel of St. Mary
at Westminster.   And here, in comfort and in peace, as
there seems every reason to believe, he died before another
year, and with it the century, had quite run out—on October 25th, 1400.

Our fancy may readily picture to itself the last days of
Geoffrey Chaucer, and the ray of autumn sunshine which
gilded his reverend head before it was bowed in death.
His old patron's more fortunate son, whose earlier chivalrous days we are apt to overlook in thinking of him as
a politic king and the sagacious founder of a dynasty, cannot have been indifferent to the welfare of a subject for
whose needs he had provided with so prompt a liberality.
In the vicinity of a throne the smiles of royalty are wont
to be contagious—and probably many a courtier thought
well to seek the company of one who, so far as we know,
had never forfeited the good-will of any patron or the
attachment of any friend.   We may, too, imagine him visited by associates who loved and honoured the poet as
well as the man—by Gower, blind, or nearly so, if tradition
speak the truth, and who, having " long had sickness upon
hand," seems, unlike Chaucer, to have been ministered to
in his old age by a housewife whom he had taken to himself in contradiction of principles preached by both the
poets ; and by "Bukton," converted, perchance, by means
of Chaucer's gift to him of the *Wife of Bath's Tale*, to a
resolution of perpetual bachelorhood, but otherwise, as Mr.
Carlyle would say, "dim to us."   Besides these, if he was
still among the living, the philosophical Strode in his Dominican habit, on a visit to London from one of his monasteries ; or—more probably—the youthful Lydgate, not yet
a Benedictine monk, but pausing, on his return from his
travels in divers lands, to sit awhile, as it were, at the feet

of the master in whose poetic example he took pride; the courtly Scogan; and Occleve, already learned, who was to cherish the memory of Chaucer's outward features as well as of his fruitful intellect: all these may in his closing days have gathered around their friend; and perhaps one or the other may have been present to close the watchful eyes for ever.

But there was yet another company with which, in these last years, and perhaps in these last days of his life, Chaucer had intercourse, of which he can rarely have lost sight, and which even in solitude he must have had constantly with him. This company has since been well known to generations and centuries of Englishmen. Its members head that goodly procession of figures which have been familiar to our fathers as live-long friends, which are the same to us, and will be to our children after us— the procession of the nation's favourites among the characters created by our great dramatists and novelists, the eternal types of human nature which nothing can efface from our imagination. Or is there less reality about the *Knight* in his short cassock and old-fashioned armour and the *Wife of Bath* in hat and wimple, than—for instance—about Uncle Toby and the Widow Wadman? Can we not hear *Madame Eglantine* lisping her "Stratford-atte-Bowe" French as if she were a personage in a comedy by Congreve or Sheridan? Is not the *Summoner*, with his "fire-red cherubim's face," a worthy companion, for Lieutenant Bardolph himself? And have not the humble *Parson* and his Brother the *Ploughman* that irresistible pathos which Dickens could find in the simple and the poor? All these figures, with those of their fellow-pilgrims, are to us living men and women; and in their midst the poet who created them lives, as he has painted

6

himself among the company, not less faithfully than Occleve depicted him from memory after death.

How long Chaucer had been engaged upon the *Canterbury Tales* it is impossible to decide.   No process is more
hazardous than that of distributing a poet's works among
the several periods of his life according to divisions of species—placing his tragedies or serious stories in one season, his comedies or lighter tales in another, and so forth.
Chaucer no more admits of such treatment than Shakspeare; nor, because there happens to be in his case little
actual evidence by which to control or contradict it, are
we justified in subjecting him to it.   All we know is that
he left his great work a fragment, and that we have no
mention in any of his other poems of more than three
of the *Tales*—two, as already noticed, being mentioned in
the Prologue to the Legend of Good Women, written at a
time when they had perhaps not yet assumed the form in
which they are preserved, while to the third (the *Wife of
Bath*) reference is made in the *Envoi to Bukton*, the date
of which is quite uncertain.   At the same time, the labour
which was expended upon the *Canterbury Tales* by their
author manifestly obliges us to conclude that their composition occupied several years, with inevitable interruptions;
while the gaiety and brightness of many of the stories,
and the exuberant humour and exquisite pathos of others, as well as the masterly effectiveness of the *Prologue*,
make it almost certain that these parts of the work were
written when Chaucer was not only capable of doing his
best, but also in a situation which admitted of his doing
it.   The supposition is, therefore, a very probable one, that
the main period of their composition may have extended
over the last eleven or twelve years of his life, and have
begun about the time when he was again placed above

want by his appointment to the Clerkship of the Royal Works.

Again, it is virtually certain that the poem of the *Canterbury Tales* was left in an unfinished and partially unconnected condition, and it is altogether uncertain whether Chaucer had finally determined upon maintaining or modifying the scheme originally indicated by him in the *Prologue*. There can, accordingly, be no necessity for working out a scheme into which everything that he has left belonging to the *Canterbury Tales* may most easily and appropriately fit. Yet the labour is by no means lost of such inquiries as those which have, with singular zeal, been prosecuted concerning the several problems that have to be solved before such a scheme can be completed. Without a review of the evidence it would, however, be preposterous to pronounce on the proper answer to be given to the questions: what were the number of tales and that of tellers ultimately designed by Chaucer; what was the order in which he intended the *Tales* actually written by him to stand; and what was the plan of the journey of his pilgrims, as to the localities of its stages and as to the time occupied by it — whether one day for the fifty-six miles from London to Canterbury (which is by no means impossible), or two days (which seems more likely), or four. The route of the pilgrimage must have been one in parts of which it is pleasant even now to dally, when the sweet spring flowers are in bloom which Mr. Boughton has painted for lovers of the poetry of English landscape.

There are one or two other points which should not be overlooked in considering the *Canterbury Tales* as a whole. It has sometimes been assumed as a matter of course that the plan of the work was borrowed from Boccaccio. If this means that Chaucer owed to the *Decam-*

erone the idea of including a number of stories in the framework of a single narrative, it implies too much. For this notion, a familiar one in the East, had long been known to Western Europe by the numerous versions of the terribly ingenious story of the *Seven Wise Masters* (in the progress of which the unexpected never happens), as well as by similar collections of the same kind. And the special connexion of this device with a company of pilgrims might, as has been well remarked, have been suggested to Chaucer by an English book certainly within his ken, the *Vision concerning Piers Plowman*, where, in the "fair field full of folk," are assembled, among others, "pilgrims and palmers who went forth on their way" to St. James of Compostella and to saints at Rome "*with many wise tales*"—("and had leave to lie all their life after"). But even had Chaucer owed the idea of his plan to Boccaccio, he would not thereby have incurred a heavy debt to the Italian novelist. There is nothing really dramatic in the schemes of the *Decamerone*, or of the numerous imitations which it called forth, from the French *Heptaméron* and the Neapolitan *Pentamerone* down to the German *Phantasus*. It is unnecessary to come nearer to our own times; for the author of the *Earthly Paradise* follows Chaucer in endeavouring at least to give a framework of real action to his collection of poetic tales. There is no organic connexion between the powerful narrative of the Plague opening Boccaccio's book, and the stories, chiefly of love and its adventures, which follow; all that Boccaccio did was to preface an interesting series of tales by a more interesting chapter of history, and then to bind the tales themselves together lightly and naturally in days, like rows of pearls in a collar. But while in the *Decamerone* the framework, in its relation to the stories, is of lit-

tle or no significance, in the *Canterbury Tales* it forms one
of the most valuable organic elements in the whole work.
One test of the distinction is this: what reader of the *Decamerone* connects any of the novels composing it with
the personality of the particular narrator, or even cares to
remember the grouping of the stories as illustrations of
fortunate or unfortunate, adventurous or illicit, passion?
The charm of Boccaccio's book, apart from the independent merits of the Introduction, lies in the admirable skill
and unflagging vivacity with which the "novels" themselves are told. The scheme of the *Canterbury Tales*, on
the other hand, possesses some genuinely dramatic elements. If the entire form, at all events in its extant condition, can scarcely be said to have a plot, it at least has
an *exposition* unsurpassed by that of any comedy, ancient
or modern; it has the possibility of a growth of action
and interest; and, which is of far more importance, it has
a variety of characters which mutually both relieve and
supplement one another. With how sure an instinct, by
the way, Chaucer has anticipated that unwritten law of
the modern drama according to which low comedy characters always appear in couples! Thus the *Miller* and the
Reeve are a noble pair running in parallel lines, though in
contrary directions; so are the *Cook* and the *Manciple*, and
again and more especially the *Friar* and the *Summoner*.
Thus at least the germ of a comedy exists in the plan of
the *Canterbury Tales*. No comedy could be formed out
of the mere circumstance of a company of ladies and gentlemen sitting down in a country-house to tell an unlim-
ited number of stories on a succession of topics; but a
comedy could be written with the purpose of showing
how a wide variety of national types will present themselves, when brought into mutual contact by an occasion

peculiarly fitted to call forth their individual rather than
their common characteristics.

For not only are we at the opening of the *Canterbury
Tales* placed in the very heart and centre of English life;
but the poet contrives to find for what may be called his
action a background, which seems of itself to suggest the
most serious emotions and the most humorous associations.
And this without anything grotesque in the collocation,
such as is involved in the notion of men telling anecdotes
at a funeral, or forgetting a pestilence over love-stories.
Chaucer's *dramatis personæ* are a company of pilgrims,
whom at first we find assembled in a hostelry in Southwark, and whom we afterwards accompany on their journey to Canterbury. The hostelry is that *Tabard* inn
which, though it changed its name, and no doubt much of
its actual structure, long remained, both in its general appearance, and perhaps in part of its actual self, a genuine
relic of mediæval London. There, till within a very few
years from the present date, might still be had a draught
of that London ale of which Chaucer's *Cook* was so thorough a *connoisseur ;* and there within the big courtyard, surrounded by a gallery very probably a copy of its predecessor, was ample room for

> ". . . Well nine and twenty in a company
> Of sundry folk,"

with their horses and travelling gear sufficient for a ride
to Canterbury. The goal of this ride has its religious, its
national, one might even say its political aspect ; but the
journey itself has an importance of its own. A journey
is generally one of the best of opportunities for bringing
out the distinctive points in the characters of travellers ;
and we are accustomed to say that no two men can long

travel in one another's company unless their friendship is
equal to the severest of tests. At home men live mostly
among colleagues and comrades; on a journey they are
placed in continual contrast with men of different pursuits
and different habits of life. The shipman away from his
ship, the monk away from his cloister, the scholar away
from his books, become interesting instead of remaining
commonplace, because the contrasts become marked which
exist between them. /Moreover, men undertake journeys
for divers purposes, and a pilgrimage in Chaucer's day
united a motley group of chance companions in search of
different ends at the same goal./ One goes to pray, the
other seeks profit; the third distraction, the fourth pleasure. . To some the road is everything; to others, its ter-
minus. All this vanity lay in the mere choice of Chaucer's framework; there was, accordingly, something of genius in the thought itself; and even an inferior workmanship could hardly have left a description of a Canterbury
pilgrimage unproductive of a wide variety of dramatic
effects.

But Chaucer's workmanship was as admirable as his
selection of his framework was felicitous. He has executed only part of his scheme, according to which each
pilgrim was to tell two tales both going and coming, and
the best narrator, the laureate of this merry company, was
to be rewarded by a supper at the common expense on
their return to their starting-place. Thus the design was,
not merely to string together a number of poetical tales
by an easy thread, but to give a real unity and completeness to the whole poem. All the tales told by all the
pilgrims were to be connected together by links; the
reader was to take an interest in the movement and
progress of the journey to and fro; and the poem was

to have a middle as well as a beginning and an end—the beginning being the inimitable *Prologue* as it now stands; the middle the history of the pilgrims' doings at Canterbury; and the close their return and farewell celebration at the Tabard inn. Though Chaucer carried out only about a fourth part of this plan, yet we can see, as clearly as if the whole poem lay before us in a completed form, that its most salient feature was intended to lie in the variety of its characters.

Each of these characters is distinctly marked out in itself, while at the same time it is designed as the type of a class. This very obvious criticism, of course, most readily admits of being illustrated by the *Prologue*—a gallery of *genre*-portraits which many master-hands have essayed to reproduce with pen or with pencil. Indeed, one lover of Chaucer sought to do so with both—poor gifted Blake, whose descriptive text of his picture of the Canterbury Pilgrims Charles Lamb, with the loving exaggeration in which he was at times fond of indulging, pronounced the finest criticism on Chaucer's poem he had ever read. But it should be likewise noticed that the character of each pilgrim is kept up through the poem, both incidentally in the connecting passages between tale and tale, and in the manner in which the tales themselves are introduced and told. The connecting passages are full of dramatic vivacity; in these the *Host*, Master Harry Bailly, acts as a most efficient *choragus;* but the other pilgrims are not silent, and in the *Manciple's* Prologue the *Cook* enacts a bit of downright farce for the amusement of the company and of stray inhabitants of "Bob-up-and-down." He is, however, homœopathically cured of the effects of his drunkenness, so that the *Host* feels justified in offering up a thanksgiving to Bacchus

for his powers of conciliation. The *Man of Law's* Prologue is an argument; the *Wife of Bath's* the ceaseless
clatter of an indomitable tongue. The sturdy *Franklin*
corrects himself when deviating into circumlocution :—

> "Till that the brightë sun had lost his hue,
> For th' hórizon had reft the sun of light
> (This is as much to say as : it was night)."

The *Miller* "tells his churlish tale in his manner," of
which manner the less said the better; while in the *Reeve's
Tale*, Chaucer even, after the manner of a comic dramatist, gives his Northern undergraduate a vulgar, ungram-
matical phraseology, probably designedly, since the poet
was himself a "Southern man." The *Pardoner* is exuberant in his sample-eloquence; the *Doctor of Physic* is grave-
ly and sententiously moral—

> "... A proper man,
> And like a prelate, by Saint Runyan,"

says the *Host*. Most sustained of all, though he tells no
tale, is, from the nature of the case, the character of Harry
Bailly, the host of the Tabard, himself — who, whatever
resemblance he may bear to his actual original, is the an-
cestor of a long line of descendants, including mine Host
of the Garter in the *Merry Wives of Windsor*. He is a
thorough worldling, to whom anything smacking of the
precisian in morals is as offensive as anything of a Romantic tone in literature ; he smells a Lollard without fail,
and turns up his nose at an old-fashioned ballad or a string
of tragic instances as out of date or tedious. In short, he
speaks his mind and that of other more timid people at
the same time, and is one of those sinners whom every-
body both likes and respects. "I advise," says the *Par-*

6*

doner, with polite impudence (when inviting the company
to become purchasers of the holy wares which he has for
sale), that

> "... Our host, he shall begin,
> For he is most envelopèd in sin."

He is thus both an admirable picture in himself and an
admirable foil to those characters which are most unlike
him—above all, to the *Parson* and the *Clerk of Oxford*,
the representatives of religion and learning.
As to the *Tales* themselves, Chaucer beyond a doubt
meant their style and tone to be above all things *popular*.
This is one of the causes accounting for the favour shown
to the work—a favour attested, so far as earlier times are
concerned, by the vast number of manuscripts existing of
it.   The *Host* is, so to speak, charged with the constant
injunction of this cardinal principle of popularity as to
both theme and style.   "Tell us," he coolly demands of
the most learned and sedate of all his fellow-travellers,

> "... Some merry thing of ádventures ;
> Your termës, your coloúrs, and your figúres,
> Keep them in store, till so be ye indite
> High style, as when that men to kingës write ;
> Speak ye so plain at this time, we you pray,
> That we may understandë that ye say."

And the *Clerk* follows the spirit of the injunction both
by omitting, as impertinent, a proeme in which his original, Petrarch, gives a great deal of valuable, but not in its
connexion interesting, geographical information, and by
adding a facetious moral to what he calls the "unrestful
matter" of his story.   Even the *Squire*, though, after the
manner of young men, far more than his elders addicted to
the grand style, and accordingly specially praised for his

eloquence by the simple *Franklin*, prefers to reduce to its plain meaning the courtly speech of the Knight of the Brazen Steed. In connexion with what was said above, it is observable that each of the *Tales* in subject suits its narrator. Not by chance is the all-but-Quixotic romance of *Palamon and Arcite*, taken by Chaucer from Boccaccio's *Teseide*, related by the *Knight;* not by chance does the *Clerk*, following Petrarch's Latin version of a story related by the same author, tell the even more improbable, but, in the plainness of its moral, infinitely more fructuous, tale of patient Griseldis. How well the *Second Nun* is fitted with a legend which carries us back a few centuries into the atmosphere of Hrosvitha's comedies, and suggests with the utmost verisimilitude the nature of a nun's lucubrations on the subject of marriage. It is impossible to go through the whole list of the *Tales;* but all may be truly said to be in keeping with the characters and manners (often equally indifferent) of their tellers—down to that of the *Nun's Priest*, which, brimful of humour as it is, has just the mild naughtiness about it which comes so drolly from a spiritual director in his worldlier hour.

Not a single one of these *Tales* can with any show of reason be ascribed to Chaucer's own invention. French literature—chiefly, though not solely, that of *fabliaux*—doubtless supplied the larger share of his materials; but that here also his debts to Italian literature, and to Boccaccio in particular, are considerable, seems hardly to admit of denial. But while Chaucer freely borrowed from foreign models, he had long passed beyond the stage of translating without assimilating. It would be rash to assume that where he altered he invariably improved. His was not the unerring eye which, like Shakspeare's in his dramatic transfusions of Plutarch, missed no particle of

the gold mingled with the baser metal, but rejected the
dross with sovereign certainty. In dealing with Italian
originals more especially, he sometimes altered for the
worse, and sometimes for the better; but he was never a
mere slavish translator. So in the *Knight's Tale* he may
be held in some points to have deviated disadvantageously
from his original; but, on the other hand, in the *Clerk's
Tale* he inserts a passage on the fidelity of women, and
another on the instability of the multitude, besides adding
a touch of nature irresistibly pathetic in the exclamation
of the faithful wife, tried beyond her power of concealing
the emotion within her:

> "O gracious God! how gentle and how kind
> Ye seemèd by your speech and your viságe
> The day that makèd was our marriáge."

So also in the *Man of Law's Tale*, which is taken from
the French, he increases the vivacity of the narrative by a
considerable number of apostrophes in his own favourite
manner, besides pleasing the general reader by divers general reflexions of his own inditing. Almost necessarily,
the literary form and the self-consistency of his originals
lose under such treatment. But his dramatic sense, on
which, perhaps, his commentators have not always sufficiently dwelt, is rarely, if ever, at fault. Two illustrations
of this gift in Chaucer must suffice, which shall be chosen
in two quarters where he has worked with materials of the
most widely different kind. Many readers must have compared with Dante's original (in canto xxxiii. of the *Infer-
no*) Chaucer's version in the *Monk's Tale* of the story of
Ugolino. Chaucer, while he necessarily omits the ghastly
introduction, expands the pathetic picture of the sufferings
of the father and his sons in their dungeon, and closes, far

more briefly and effectively than Dante, with a touch of
the most refined pathos:—

"DE HUGILINO COMITE PISÆ.

" Of Hugolin of Pisa the languór
    There may no tonguë tellë for pity.
But little out of Pisa stands a tower,
    In whichë tower in prison put was he;
    And with him be his little children three.
The eldest scarcely five years was of age;
    Alas! fortúne! it was great cruelty
Such birds as these to put in such a cage.

" Condemned he was to die in that prisón,
    For Royer, which that bishop was of Pise,
Had on him made a false suggestión,
    Through which the people gan on him arise,
    And put him in prisón in such a wise,
As ye have heard, and meat and drink he had
    So little that it hardly might suffice,
And therewithal it was full poor and bad.

" And on a day befell that in that hour
    When that his meat was wont to be y-brought,
The gaoler shut the doorës of that tower.
    He heard it well, although he saw it not;
    And in his heart anon there fell a thought
That they his death by hunger did devise.
    ' Alas!' quoth he—' alas! that I was wrought!'
Therewith the tearës fellë from his eyes.

" His youngest son, that three years was of age,
    Unto him said: ' Father, why do ye weep?
When will the gaoler bring us our pottáge?
    Is there no morsel bread that ye do keep?
    I am so hungry that I cannot sleep.
Now wouldë God that I might sleep for ever!
    Then should not hunger in my belly creep.
There is no thing save bread that I would liever."

> " Thus day by day this child began to cry,
>   Till in his father's lap adown he lay,
>   And saidë : ' Farewell, father, I must die!'
>   And kissed his father, and died the samë day.
>   The woeful father saw that dead he lay,
>   And his two arms for woe began to bite,
>   And said : ' Fortune, alas and well-away !
>   For all my woe I blame thy treacherous spite.'
>
> " His children weened that it for hunger was,
>   That he his armës gnawed, and not for woe.
>   And saidë : ' Father, do not so, alas !
>   But rather eat the flesh upon us two.
>   Our flesh thou gavest us, our flesh thou take us fro,
>   And eat enough.'   Right thus they to him cried ;
>   And after that, within a day or two,
>   They laid them in his lap adown and died."

The father, in despair, likewise died of hunger ; and such
was the end of the mighty Earl of Pisa, whose tragedy
whosoever desires to hear at greater length may read it as
told by the great poet of Italy hight Dante.

The other instance is that of *The Pardoner's Tale*, which
would appear to have been based on a *fabliau* now lost,
though the substance of it is preserved in an Italian novel,
and in one or two other versions. For the purpose of noticing how Chaucer arranges as well as tells a story, the
following attempt at a condensed prose rendering of his
narrative may be acceptable :—

Once upon a time in Flanders there was a company of
young men, who gave themselves up to every kind of
dissipation and debauchery—haunting the taverns where
dancing and dicing continues day and night, eating and
drinking, and serving the devil in his own temple by their
outrageous life of luxury.   It was horrible to hear their
oaths, how they tore to pieces our blessed Lord's body, as

if they thought the Jews had not rent Him enough; and each laughed at the sin of the others, and all were alike immersed in gluttony and wantonness.

And so one morning it befel that three of these rioters were sitting over their drink in a tavern, long before the bell had rung for nine-o'clock prayers. And as they sat, they heard a bell clinking before a corpse that was being carried to the grave. So one of them bade his servant-lad go and ask what was the name of the dead man; but the boy said that he knew it already, and that it was the name of an old companion of his master's. As he had been sitting drunk on a bench, there had come a privy thief, whom men called Death, and who slew all the people in this country; and he had smitten the drunken man's heart in two with his spear, and had then gone on his way without any more words. This Death had slain a thousand during the present pestilence; and the boy thought it worth warning his master to beware of such an adversary, and to be ready to meet him at any time. "So my mother taught me; I say no more." "Marry," said the keeper of the tavern; "the child tells the truth: this Death has slain all the inhabitants of a great village not far from here; I think that there must be the place where he dwells." Then the rioter swore with some of his big oaths that he at least was not afraid of this Death, and that he would seek him out wherever he dwelt. And at his instance his two boon-companions joined with him in a vow that before nightfall they would slay the false traitor Death, who was the slayer of so many; and the vow they swore was one of closest fellowship between them— to live and die for one another as if they had been brethren born. And so they went forth in their drunken fury towards the village of which the taverner had spoken, with terrible execrations on their lips that "Death should be dead, if they might catch him."

They had not gone quite half a mile when, at a stile between two fields, they came upon a poor old man, who meekly greeted them with a "God save you, sirs." But the proudest of the three rioters answered him roughly, asking him why he kept himself all wrapped up except his face, and how so old a fellow as he had managed to keep alive so long? And the old man looked him straight in the face and replied, "Because in no town or village, though I journey as far as the Indies, can I find a man willing to exchange his youth for my age; and therefore I must keep it so long as God wills it so. Death, alas! will not have my life, and so I wander about like a restless fugitive, and early and late I knock on the ground, which is my mother's gate, with my staff, and say, 'Dear mother, let me in! behold how I waste away! Alas! when shall my bones be at rest? Mother, gladly will I give you my chest containing all my worldly gear in return for a shroud to wrap me in.' But she refuses me that grace, and that is why my face is pale and withered. But you, sirs, are uncourteous to speak rudely to an inoffensive old man, when Holy Writ bids you reverence grey hairs. Therefore, never again give offence to an old man, if you wish men to be courteous to you in your age, should you live so long. And so God be with you; I must go whither I have to go." But the second rioter prevented him, and swore he should not depart so lightly. "Thou spakest just now of that traitor Death, who slays all our friends in this country. As thou art his spy, hear me swear that, unless thou tellest where he is, thou shalt die; for thou art in his plot to slay us young men, thou false thief!" Then the old man told them that if they were so desirous

of finding Death, they had but to turn up a winding path
to which he pointed, and there they would find him they
sought in a grove under an oak-tree, where the old man
had just left him; "he will not try to hide himself for all
your boasting. And so may God the Redeemer save you
and amend you!" And when he had spoken, all the three
rioters ran till they came to the tree. But what they found
there was a treasure of golden florins—nearly seven bush-
els of them, as they thought. Then they no longer sought
after Death, but sat down all three by the shining gold.
And the youngest of them spoke first, and declared that
Fortune had given this treasure to them, so that they might
spend the rest of their lives in mirth and jollity. The
question was how to take this money—which clearly belonged to some one else—safely to the house of one of the
three companions. It must be done by night; so let them
draw lots, and let him on whom the lot fell run to the
town to fetch bread and wine, while the other two guard-
ed the treasure carefully till the night came, when they
might agree whither to transport it.

The lot fell on the youngest, who forthwith went his
way to the town. Then one of those who remained with
the treasure said to the other: "Thou knowest well that
thou art my sworn brother, and I will tell thee something
to thy advantage. Our companion is gone, and here is a
great quantity of gold to be divided among us three. But
say, if I could manage so that the gold is divided between
us two, should I not do thee a friend's turn?" And when
the other failed to understand him, he made him promise
secrecy, and disclosed his plan. "Two are stronger than
one. When he sits down, arise as if thou wouldest sport
with him; and while thou art struggling with him as in
play, I will rive him through both his sides; and look

thou do the same with thy dagger. After which, my dear friend, we will divide all the gold between you and me, and then we may satisfy all our desires and play at dice to our hearts' content."

Meanwhile the youngest rioter, as he went up to the town, revolved in his heart the beauty of the bright new florins, and said unto himself : "If only I could have all this gold to myself alone, there is no man on earth who would live so merrily as I." And at last the Devil put it into his relentless heart to buy poison, in order with it to kill his two companions. And straightway he went on into the town to an apothecary, and besought him to sell him some poison for destroying some rats which infested his house, and a polecat which, he said, had made away with his capons. And the apothecary said : "Thou shalt have something of which (so may God save my soul!) no creature in all the world could swallow a single grain without losing his life thereby—and that in less time than thou wouldest take to walk a mile in." So the miscreant shut up this poison in a box, and then he went into the next street and borrowed three large bottles, into two of which he poured his poison, while the third he kept clean to hold drink for himself ; for he meant to work hard all the night to carry away the gold. So he filled his three bottles with wine, and then went back to his companions under the tree.

What need to make a long discourse of what followed? As they had plotted their comrade's death, so they slew him, and that at once. And when they had done this, the one who had counselled the deed said, " Now let us sit and drink and make merry, and then we will bury his body." And it happened to him by chance to take one of the bottles which contained the poison ; and he drank, and gave drink of it to his fellow; and thus they both speedily died.

The plot of this story is, as observed, not Chaucer's. But how carefully, how artistically, the narrative is elaborated, incident by incident, and point by point! How well every effort is prepared, and how well every turn of the story is explained! Nothing is superfluous, but everything is arranged with care, down to the circumstances of the bottles being bought, for safety's sake, in the next street to the apothecary's, and of two out of three bottles being filled with poison, which is at once a proceeding natural in itself, and increases the chances against the two rioters when they are left to choose for themselves. This it is to be a good story-teller. But of a different order is the change introduced by Chaucer into his original, where the old hermit—who, of course, is Death himself—is fleeing from Death. Chaucer's Old Man is *seeking* Death, but seeking him in vain—like the Wandering Jew of the legend. This it is to be a poet.

Of course it is always necessary to be cautious before asserting any apparent addition of Chaucer's to be his own invention. Thus, in the *Merchant's Tale*, the very naughty plot of which is anything but original, it is impossible to say whether such is the case with the humorous competition of advice between Justinus and Placebo,[1] or with the fantastic machinery in which Pluto and Proserpine anticipate the part played by Oberon and Titania in *A Midsummer Night's Dream*. On the other hand, Chaucer is capable of using goods manifestly borrowed or stolen for

[1] "Placebo" seems to have been a current term to express the character or the ways of "the too deferential man." "Flatterers be the Devil's chaplains, that sing aye *Placebo*."—*Parson's Tale*.

a purpose never intended in their original employment.
Puck himself must have guided the audacious hand which
could turn over the leaves of so respected a Father of the
Church as St. Jerome, in order to derive from his treatise
On Perpetual Virginity materials for the discourse on
matrimony delivered, with illustrations essentially her own,
by the *Wife of Bath*.

Two only among these *Tales* are in prose—a vehicle of
expression, on the whole, strange to the polite literature
of the pre-Renascence ages—but not both for the same
reason. The first of these *Tales* is told by the poet himself, after a stop has been unceremoniously put upon his
recital of the *Ballad of Sir Thopas* by the Host. The
ballad itself is a fragment of straightforward burlesque,
which shows that in both the manner and the metre[1] of
ancient romances, literary criticism could even in Chaucer's
days find its opportunities for satire, though it is going
rather far to see in *Sir Thopas* a predecessor of *Don
Quixote*. The *Tale of Meliboeus* is probably an English
version of a French translation of Albert of Brescia's famous *Book of Consolation and Counsel*, which comprehends
in a slight narrative framework a long discussion between
the unfortunate Meliboeus, whom the wrongs and sufferings inflicted upon him and his have brought to the verge
of despair, and his wise helpmate, Dame Prudence. By
means of a long argumentation propped up by quotations
(not invariably assigned with conscientious accuracy to
their actual source) from "The Book," Seneca, "Tullius,"
and other authors, she at last persuades him not only to
reconcile himself to his enemies, but to forgive them, even
as he hopes to be forgiven. And thus the Tale well bears

[1] Dunbar's burlesque ballad of *Sir Thomas Norray* is in the same
stanza.

out the truth impressed upon Meliboeus by the following ingeniously combined quotation :—

And there said once a clerk in two verses : What is better than gold? Jasper. And what is better than jasper? Wisdom. And what is better than wisdom? Woman. And what is better than woman? No thing.

Certainly, Chaucer gave proof of consummate tact and taste, as well as of an unaffected personal modesty, in assigning to himself as one of the company of pilgrims, instead of a tale bringing him into competition with the creatures of his own invention, after his mocking ballad has served its turn, nothing more ambitious than a version of a popular discourse — half narrative, half homily — in prose. But a question of far greater difficulty and moment arises with regard to the other prose piece included among the *Canterbury Tales*.. Of these the so-called *Parson's Tale* is the last in order of succession. Is it to be looked upon as an integral part of the collection ; and, if so, what general and what personal significance should be attached to it ?

As it stands, the long tractate or sermon (partly adapted from a popular French religious manual), which bears the name of the *Parson's Tale*, is, if not unfinished, at least internally incomplete. It lacks symmetry, and fails entirely to make good the argument or scheme of divisions with which the sermon begins, as conscientiously as one of Barrow's. Accordingly, an attempt has been made to show that what we have is something different from the "meditation" which Chaucer originally put into his *Parson's* mouth. But, while we may stand in respectful awe of the German daring which, whether the matter in hand be a few pages of Chaucer, a Book of Homer, or a chapter of the Old Testament, is fully prepared to show which parts of each are mutilated, which interpolated, and which transposed, we may safely content ourselves, in the present instance, with considering the preliminary question. *A priori*, is there sufficient reason for supposing any transpositions, interpolations, and mutilations to have been introduced into the *Parson's Tale?* The question is full of interest; for while, on the one hand, the character of the *Parson* in the *Prologue* has been frequently interpreted as evidence of sympathy on Chaucer's part with Wycliffism, on the other hand the *Parson's Tale*, in its extant form, goes far to disprove the supposition that its author was a Wycliffite.

This, then, seems the appropriate place for briefly reviewing the vexed question — *Was Chaucer a Wycliffite?* Apart from the character of the *Parson* and from the *Parson's Tale*, what is the nature of our evidence on the subject? In the first place, nothing could be clearer than that Chaucer was a very free-spoken critic of the life of the clergy—more especially of the Regular clergy—of his times. In this character he comes before us from his translation of the *Roman de la Rose* to the *Parson's Tale* itself, where he inveighs with significant earnestness against self-indulgence on the part of those who are Religious, or have "entered into Orders, as sub-deacon, or deacon, or priest, or hospitallers." In the *Canterbury Tales*, above all, his attacks upon the Friars run nearly the whole gamut of satire, stopping short, perhaps, before the note of high moral indignation. Moreover, as has been seen, his long connexion with John of Gaunt is a well-established fact; and it has thence been concluded that Chaucer fully shared the opinions and tendencies represented by his patron. In the supposition that Chaucer approved of the

countenance for a long time shown by John of Gaunt to
Wyclif there is nothing improbable; neither, however, is
there anything improbable in this other supposition, that,
when the Duke of Lancaster openly washed his hands of
the heretical tenets to the utterance of which Wyclif had
advanced, Chaucer, together with the large majority of
Englishmen, held with the politic duke rather than with
the still unflinching Reformer. So long as Wyclif's movement consisted only of an opposition to ecclesiastical pretensions on the one hand, and of an attempt to revive religious sentiment on the other, half the country or more
was Wycliffite, and Chaucer no doubt with the rest. But
it would require positive evidence to justify the belief that
from this feeling Chaucer ever passed to sympathy with
Lollardry, in the vague but sufficiently intelligible sense
attaching to that term in the latter part of Richard the
Second's reign. Richard II. himself, whose patronage of
Chaucer is certain, in the end attempted rigorously to
suppress Lollardry; and Henry IV., the politic John of
Gaunt's yet more politic son, to whom Chaucer owed the
prosperity enjoyed by him in the last year of his life, became a persecutor almost as soon as he became a king.

Though, then, from the whole tone of his mind, Chaucer could not but sympathise with the opponents of ecclesiastical domination—though, as a man of free and critical spirit, and of an inborn ability for penetrating beneath
the surface, he could not but find subjects for endless
blame and satire in the members of those Mendicant Orders in whom his chief patron's academical ally had recognised the most formidable obstacles to the spread of
pure religion—yet all this would not justify us in regarding him as personally a Wycliffite. Indeed, we might as
well at once borrow the phraseology of a recent respect-

able critic, and set down Dan Chaucer as a Puritan! The policy of his patron tallied with the view which a fresh practical mind such as Chaucer's would naturally be disposed to take of the influence of monks and friars, or at least of those monks and friars whose vices and foibles were specially prominent in his eyes. There are various reasons why men oppose established institutions in the season of their decay; but a fourteenth-century satirist of the monks, or even of the clergy at large, was not necessarily a Lollard, any more than a nineteenth-century objector to doctors' drugs is necessarily a homœopathist.

But, it is argued by some, Chaucer has not only assailed the false; he has likewise extolled the true. He has painted both sides of the contrast. On the one side are the Monk, the Friar, and the rest of their fellows; on the other is the *Poor Parson of a Town*—a portrait, if not of Wyclif himself, at all events of a Wycliffite priest; and in the *Tale* or sermon put in the Parson's mouth are recognisable beneath the accumulations of interested editors some of the characteristic marks of Wycliffism. Who is not acquainted with the exquisite portrait in question?—

> "A good man was there of religión,
> And was a poorë Parson of a town.
> But rich he was of holy thought and work.
> He was also a learnèd man, a clerk
> That Christës Gospel truly wouldë preach;
> And his parishioners devoutly teach.
> Benign he was, and wondrous diligent,
> And in adversity full patiént.
> And such he was y-provèd oftë sithes.
> Full loth he was to curse men for his tithes;
> But rather would he givë, without doubt,
> Unto his poor parishioners about
> Of his off'ríng and eke of his substánce.
> He could in little wealth have súffisance.

Wide was his parish, houses far asunder,
Yet failed he not for either rain or thunder
In sickness nor mischance to visit all
The furthest in his parish, great and small,
Upon his feet, and in his hand a staff.
This noble ensample to his sheep he gave,
That first he wrought, and afterwards he taught;
Out of the Gospel he those wordës caught;
And this figúre he added eke thereto,
That ' if gold rustë, what shall iron do ?'
For if a priest be foul, on whom we trust,
No wonder is it if a layman rust;
And shame it is, if that a priest take keep,
A foul shepherd to see and a clean sheep;
Well ought a priest ensample for to give
By his cleannéss, how that his sheep should live.
He put not out his benefice on hire,
And left his sheep encumbered in the mire,
And ran to London unto Saintë Paul's,
To seek himself a chantery for souls,
Or maintenance with a brotherhood to hold;
But dwelt at home, and keptë well his fold,
So that the wolf ne'er made it to miscarry;
He was a shepherd and no mercenáry.
And though he holy were, and virtuous,
He was to sinful man not déspitous,
And of his speech nor difficult nor digne,
But in his teaching díscreet and benign.
For to draw folk to heaven by fairnéss,
By good ensample, this was his business:
But were there any person obstinate,
What so he were, of high or low estate,
Him would he sharply snub at once.   Than this
A better priest, I trow, there nowhere is.
He waited for no pomp and reverence,
Nor made himself a spicèd consciénce;
But Christës lore and His Apostles' twelve
He taught, but first he followed it himself."

7

The most striking features in this portrait are undoubtedly those which are characteristics of the good and humble working clergyman of all times; and some of these, accordingly, Goldsmith could appropriately borrow for his gentle poetic sketch of his parson-brother in "Sweet Auburn." But there are likewise points in the sketch which may be fairly described as specially distinctive of Wyclif's Simple Priests—though, as should be pointed out, these Priests could not themselves be designated parsons of towns. Among the latter features are the specially evangelical source of the *Parson's* learning and teaching; and his outward appearance—the wandering, staff in hand, which was specially noted in an archiepiscopal diatribe against these novel ministers of the people. Yet it seems unnecessary to conclude anything beyond this: that the feature which Chaucer desired above all to mark and insist upon in his *Parson*, was the poverty and humility which in him contrasted with the luxurious self-indulgence of the *Monk*, and the blatant insolence of the *Pardoner*. From this point of view it is obvious why the *Parson* is made brother to the *Ploughman*; for, in drawing the latter, Chaucer cannot have forgotten that other Ploughman whom Langland's poem had identified with Him for whose sake Chaucer's poor workman laboured for his poor neighbours, with the readiness always shown by the best of his class. Nor need this recognition of the dignity of the lowly surprise us in Chaucer, who had both sense of justice and sense of humour enough not to flatter one class at the expense of the rest, and who elsewhere (in the *Manciple's Tale*) very forcibly puts the truth that what in a great man is called a *coup d'état* is called by a much simpler name in a humbler fellow-sinner.

But though, in the *Parson of a Town*, Chaucer may not

have wished to paint a Wycliffite priest—still less a Lollard, under which designation so many varieties of malcontents, in addition to the followers of Wyclif, were popularly included—yet his eyes and ears were open; and he knew well enough what the world and its children are at all times apt to call those who are not ashamed of their religion, as well as those who make too conscious a profession of it. The world called them Lollards at the close of the fourteenth century, and it called them Puritans at the close of the sixteenth, and Methodists at the close of the eighteenth. Doubtless the vintners and the shipmen of Chaucer's day, the patrons and purveyors of the playhouse in Ben Jonson's, the fox-hunting squires and town wits of Cowper's, like their successors after them, were not specially anxious to distinguish nicely between more or less abominable varieties of saintliness. Hence, when Master Harry Bailly's tremendous oaths produce the gentlest of protests from the *Parson*, the jovial *Host* incontinently "smells a Lollard in the wind," and predicts (with a further flow of expletives) that there is a sermon to follow. Whereupon the *Shipman* protests not less characteristically :—

> "'Nay, by my father's soul, that shall he not,'
> Saidë the Shipman; 'here shall he not preach:
> He shall no gospel here explain or teach.
> We all believe in the great God,' quoth he;
> 'He wouldë sowë some difficulty,
> Or springë cockle in our cleanë corn.'" [1]

After each of the pilgrims except the *Parson* has told a tale (so that obviously Chaucer designed one of the divisions of his work to close with the *Parson's*), he is again

---

[1] The nickname Lollards was erroneously derived from *lolia* (tares).

called upon by the *Host*.   Hereupon appealing to the undoubtedly evangelical and, it might without straining be
said, Wycliffite authority of Timothy, he promises as his
contribution a "merry tale in prose," which proves to consist of a moral discourse.   In its extant form the *Parson's
Tale* contains, by the side of much that might suitably
have come from a Wycliffite teacher, much of a directly
opposite nature.   For not only is the necessity of certain
sacramental usages to which Wyclif strongly objected in-
sisted upon, but the spoliation of Church property is unct-
uously inveighed against as a species of one of the cardinal sins.   No enquiry could satisfactorily establish how
much of this was taken over or introduced into the *Parson's Tale* by Chaucer himself.   But one would fain at
least claim for him a passage in perfect harmony with the
character drawn of the *Parson* in the *Prologue*—a passage
(already cited in part in the opening section of the present
essay) where the poet advocates the cause of the poor in
words which, simple as they are, deserve to be quoted side
by side with that immortal character itself.   The concluding lines may therefore be cited here :—

"Think also that of the same seed of which churls spring, of the
same seed spring lords ; as well may the churl be saved as the lord.
Wherefore I counsel thee, do just so with thy churl as thou wouldest
thy lord did with thee, if thou wert in his plight.   A very sinful man
is a churl as towards sin.   I counsel thee certainly, thou lord, that
thou work in such wise with thy churls that they rather love thee
than dread thee.   I know well, where there is degree above degree,
it is reasonable that men should do their duty where it is due ; but
of a certainty, extortions, and despite of our underlings, are damnable."

In sum, the *Parson's Tale* cannot, any more than the
character of the *Parson* in the *Prologue*, be interpreted as
proving Chaucer to have been a Wycliffite.   But the one

as well as the other proves him to have perceived much of
what was noblest in the Wycliffite movement, and much
of what was ignoblest in the reception with which it met
at the hands of worldlings — before, with the aid of the
State, the Church finally succeeded in crushing it, to all
appearance, out of existence.

The *Parson's Tale* contains a few vigorous touches, in
addition to the fine passage quoted, which make it difficult to deny that Chaucer's hand was concerned in it.
The inconsistency between the religious learning ascribed
to the *Parson* and a passage in the *Tale*, where the author
leaves certain things to be settled by divines, will not be
held of much account.   The most probable conjecture
seems, therefore, to be that the discourse has come down
to us in a mutilated form.   This *may* be due to the *Tale*
having remained unfinished at the time of Chaucer's death;
in which case it would form last words of no unfitting
kind.   As for the actual last words of the *Canterbury
Tales* — the so-called *Prayer of Chaucer* — it would be
unbearable to have to accept them as genuine.   For in
these the poet, while praying for the forgiveness of sins,
is made specially to entreat the Divine pardon for his
"translations and inditing in worldly vanities," which he
"revokes in his retractions."   These include, besides the
Book of the Leo (doubtless a translation or adaptation
from Machault) and many other books which the writer
forgets, and "many a song and many a lecherous lay,"
all the principal poetical works of Chaucer (with the
exception of the *Romaunt of the Rose*) discussed in this
essay.   On the other hand, he offers thanks for having
had the grace given him to compose his translation of
Boëthius and other moral and devotional works.   There
is, to be sure, no actual evidence to decide in either way

the question as to the genuineness of this *Prayer*, which is entirely one of internal probability. Those who will may believe that the monks, who were the landlords of Chaucer's house at Westminster, had in one way or the other obtained a controlling influence over his mind. Stranger things than this have happened; but one prefers to believe that the poet of the *Canterbury Tales* remained master of himself to the last. He had written much which a dying man might regret; but it would be sad to have to think that, "because of humility," he bore false witness at the last against an immortal part of himself—his poetic genius.

CHAPTER III.

THUS, then, Chaucer had passed away — whether in good or in evil odour with the powerful interest with which John of Gaunt's son had entered into his unwritten concordate, after all, matters but little now. He is no dim shadow to us, even in his outward presence; for we possess sufficient materials from which to picture to ourselves with good assurance what manner of man he was. Occleve painted from memory, on the margin of one of his own works, a portrait of his "worthy master," over against a passage in which, after praying the Blessed Virgin to intercede for the eternal happiness of one who had written so much in her honour, he proceeds as follows:—

> "Although his life be quenched, the résemblance
> Of him hath in me so fresh liveliness,
> That to put other men in rémembrance
> Of his persón I have here his likenéss
> Made, to this end in very soothfastness,
> That they that have of him lost thought and mind
> May by the painting here again him find."

In this portrait, in which the experienced eye of Sir Harris Nicolas sees "incomparably the best portrait of Chaucer yet discovered," he appears as an elderly rather than aged man, clad in dark gown and hood—the latter of the

fashion so familiar to us from this very picture, and from
the well-known one of Chaucer's last patron, King Henry
IV. His attitude in this likeness is that of a quiet talker,
with downcast eyes, but sufficiently erect bearing of body.
One arm is extended, and seems to be gently pointing
some observation which has just issued from the poet's
lips. The other holds a rosary, which may be significant
of the piety attributed to Chaucer by Occleve, or may be
a mere ordinary accompaniment of conversation, as it is in
parts of Greece to the present day. The features are mild
but expressive, with just a suspicion — certainly no more
—of saturnine or sarcastic humour. The lips are full, and
the nose is what is called good by the learned in such matters. Several other early portraits of Chaucer exist, all of
which are stated to bear much resemblance to one another. Among them is one in an early if not contemporary copy of Occleve's poems, full-length, and superscribed
by the hand which wrote the manuscript. In another,
which is extremely quaint, he appears on horseback, in
commemoration of his ride to Canterbury, and is represented as short of stature, in accordance with the description of himself in the *Canterbury Tales.*

For, as it fortunately happens, he has drawn his likeness
for us with his own hand, as he appeared on the occasion
to that most free-spoken of observers and most personal of
critics, the host of the Tabard, the "cock" and marshal
of the company of pilgrims. The fellow-travellers had
just been wonderfully sobered (as well they might be) by
the piteous tale of the Prioress concerning the little cler-
gy-boy—how, after the wicked Jews had cut his throat because he ever sang *O Alma Redemptoris*, and had cast him
into a pit, he was found there by his mother loudly giving
forth the hymn in honour of the Blessed Virgin which he

had loved so well. Master Harry Bailly was, as in duty bound, the first to interrupt by a string of jests the silence which had ensued:—

> " And then at first he lookèd upon me,
> And saidë thus : ' What man art thou?' quoth he ;
> ' Thou lookèst as thou wouldèst find a hare,
> For ever upon the ground I see thee stare.
> Approach more near, and lookë merrily !
> Now 'ware you, sirs, and let this man have space.
> He in the waist is shaped as well as I ;
> This were a puppet in an arm to embrace
> For any woman, small and fair of face.
> He seemeth elfish by his countenance,
> For unto no wight doth he dalliánce.' "

From this passage we may gather, not only that Chaucer was, as the *Host* of the Tabard's transparent self-irony implies, small of stature and slender, but that he was accustomed to be twitted on account of the abstracted or absent look which so often tempts children of the world to offer its wearer a penny for his thoughts. For " elfish " means bewitched by the elves, and hence vacant or absent in demeanour.

It is thus, with a few modest but manifestly truthful touches, that Chaucer, after the manner of certain great painters, introduces his own figure into a quiet corner of his crowded canvas. But mere outward likeness is of little moment, and it is a more interesting enquiry whether there are any personal characteristics of another sort, which it is possible with safety to ascribe to him, and which must be, in a greater or less degree, connected with the distinctive qualities of his literary genius ; for in truth it is but a sorry makeshift of literary biographers to seek to divide a man who is an author into two separate be-

7*

ings, in order to avoid the conversely fallacious procedure
of accounting for everything which an author has written by something which the *man* has done or been inclined to do. What true poet has sought to hide, or succeeded in hiding, his moral nature from his muse? None
in the entire band, from Petrarch to Villon, and least of all
the poet whose song, like so much of Chaucer's, seems
freshly derived from Nature's own inspiration.

One very pleasing quality in Chaucer must have been
his modesty. In the course of his life this may have
helped to recommend him to patrons so many and so various, and to make him the useful and trustworthy agent
that he evidently became for confidential missions abroad.
Physically, as has been seen, he represents himself as prone
to the habit of casting his eyes on the ground; and we
may feel tolerably sure that to this external manner corre-
sponded a quiet, observant disposition, such as that which
may be held to have distinguished the greatest of Chaucer's successors among English poets. To us, of course,
this quality of modesty in Chaucer makes itself principal-
ly manifest in the opinion which he incidentally shows
himself to entertain concerning his own rank and claims as
an author. Herein, as in many other points, a contrast is
noticeable between him and the great Italian masters, who
were so sensitive as to the esteem in which they and their
poetry were held. Who could fancy Chaucer crowned
with laurel, like Petrarch, or even, like Dante, speaking
with proud humility of "the beautiful style that has done
honour to him," while acknowledging his obligation for it
to a great predecessor? Chaucer again and again disclaims
all boasts of perfection, or pretensions to pre-eminence, as
a poet. His Canterbury Pilgrims have in his name to
disavow, like Persius, having slept on Mount Parnassus, or

possessing "rhetoric" enough to describe a heroine's beauty; and he openly allows that his spirit grows dull as he grows older, and that he finds a difficulty as a translator in matching his rhymes to his French original. He acknowledges as incontestable the superiority of the poets of classical antiquity :—

> ". . . Little book, no writing thou envy,
> But subject be to all true poësy,
> And kiss the steps, where'er thou seest space
> Of Virgil, Ovid, Homer, Lucan, Stace."[1]

But more than this. In the *House of Fame* he expressly disclaims having in his light and imperfect verse sought to pretend to "mastery" in the art poetical; and in a charmingly expressed passage of the *Prologue* to the *Legend of Good Women* he describes himself as merely following in the wake of those who have already reaped the harvest of amorous song, and have carried away the corn :—

> "And I come after, gleaning here and there,
> And am full glad if I can find an ear
> Of any goodly word that ye have left."

Modesty of this stamp is perfectly compatible with a certain self-consciousness which is hardly ever absent from greatness, and which at all events supplies a stimulus not easily dispensed with except by sustained effort on the part of a poet. The two qualities seem naturally to combine into that self-containedness (very different from self-contentedness) which distinguishes Chaucer, and which helps to give to his writings a manliness of tone, the direct opposite of the irretentive querulousness found in so great a number of poets in all times. He cannot, indeed,

[1] Statius.

be said to maintain an absolute reserve concerning himself
and his affairs in his writings; but as he grows older, he
seems to become less and less inclined to take the public
into his confidence, or to speak of himself except in a pleasantly light and incidental fashion.   And in the same spirit
he seems, without ever folding his hands in his lap, or
ceasing to be a busy man and an assiduous author, to have
grown indifferent to the lack of brilliant success in life,
whether as a man of letters or otherwise.   So at least one
seems justified in interpreting a remarkable passage in the
House of Fame, the poem in which, perhaps, Chaucer allows us to see more deeply into his mind than in any
other.   After surveying the various company of those who
had come as suitors for the favours of Fame, he tells us
how it seemed to him (in his long December dream) that
some one spoke to him in a kindly way,

> "And saidë: 'Friend, what is thy name?
> Art thou come hither to have fame?'
> 'Nay, forsoothë, friend!' quoth I;
> 'I came not hither (grand merci!)
> For no such causë, by my head!
> Sufficeth me, as I were dead,
> That no wight have my name in hand.
> I wot myself best how I stand;
> For what I suffer, or what I think,
> I will myselfë all it drink,
> Or at least the greater part
> As far forth as I know my art.' "

With this modest but manly self-possession we shall
not go far wrong in connecting what seems another very
distinctly marked feature of Chaucer's inner nature.   He
seems to have arrived at a clear recognition of the truth
with which Goethe humorously comforted Eckermann in
the shape of the proverbial saying, "Care has been taken

that the trees shall not grow into the sky." Chaucer's, there is every reason to believe, was a contented faith, as far removed from self-torturing unrest as from childish credulity. Hence his refusal to trouble himself, now that he has arrived at a good age, with original research as to the constellations. (The passage is all the more significant since Chaucer, as has been seen, actually possessed a very respectable knowledge of astronomy.) That winged encyclopædia, the Eagle, has just been regretting the poet's unwillingness to learn the position of the Great and the Little Bear, Castor and Pollux, and the rest, concerning which at present he does not know where they stand. But he replies, "No matter!

> " '. . . It is no need;
> I trust as well (so God me speed!)
> Them that write of this mattér,
> As though I knew their places there.' "

Moreover, as he says (probably without implying any special allegorical meaning), they seem so bright that it would destroy my eyes to look upon them. Personal inspection, in his opinion, was not necessary for a faith which at some times may, and at others must, take the place of knowledge; for we find him, at the opening of the *Prologue* to the *Legend of Good Women*, in a passage the tone of which should not be taken to imply less than its words express, writing as follows:—

> "A thousand timës I have heard men tell,
>   That there is joy in heaven, and pain in hell;
>   And I accordë well that it is so.
>   But nathëless, yet wot I well alsó,
>   That there is none doth in this country dwell
>   That either hath in heaven been or hell,

> Or any other way could of it know,
> But that he heard, or found it written so,
> For by assay may no man proof receive.
>   But God forbid that men should not believe
> More things than they have ever seen with eye!
> Men shall not fancy everything a lie
> Unless themselves it see, or else it do;
> For, God wot, not the less a thing is true,
> Though every wight may not it chance to see."

The central thought of these lines, though it afterwards
receives a narrower and more commonplace application,
is no other than that which has been so splendidly expressed by Spenser in the couplet :—

> "Why then should witless man so much misween
> That nothing is but that which he hath seen ?"

The *negative* result produced in Chaucer's mind by this
firm but placid way of regarding matters of faith was a
distrust of astrology, alchemy, and all the superstitions
which in the *Parson's Tale* are noticed as condemned by
the Church.   This distrust on Chaucer's part requires no
further illustration after what has been said elsewhere; it
would have been well for his age if all its children had
been as clear-sighted in these matters as he, to whom the
practices connected with these delusive sciences seemed,
and justly so from his point of view, not less impious
than futile.   His *Canon Yeoman's Tale*, a story of im-
posture so vividly dramatic in its catastrophe as to have
suggested to Ben Jonson one of the most effective passages in his comedy *The Alchemist*, concludes with a moral
of unmistakeable solemnity against the sinfulness, as well
as uselessness, of "multiplying" (making gold by the arts
of alchemy) :—

> " . . . Whoso maketh God his adversáry,
> As for to work anything in contràry
> Unto His will, certes ne'er shall he thrive,
> Though that he multiply through all his life."

But equally unmistakeable is the *positive* side of this
frame of mind in such a passage as the following—which
is one of those belonging to Chaucer himself, and not
taken from his French original—in *The Man of Law's
Tale*. The narrator is speaking of the voyage of Constance, after her escape from the massacre in which, at a
feast, all her fellow-Christians had been killed, and of how
she was borne by the " wild wave " from " Surrey " (Syria)
to the Northumbrian shore:—

> " Here men might askë, why she was not slain?
> Eke at the feast who might her body save?
> And I answérë that demand again:
> Who savèd Daniel in th' horríble cave,
> When every wight save him, master or knave,
> The lion ate—before he could depart?
> No wight but God, whom he bare in his heart."

" In her," he continues, " God desired to show His miraculous power, so that we should see His mighty works;
for Christ, in whom we have a remedy for every ill, often
by means of His own does things for ends of His own,
which are obscure to the wit of man, incapable, by reason
of our ignorance, of understanding His wise providence.
But since Constance was not slain at the feast, it might be
asked: Who kept her from drowning in the sea? Who,
then, kept Jonas in the belly of the whale till he was
spouted up at Ninive? Well do we know it was no one
but He who kept the Hebrew people from drowning in
the waters, and made them to pass through the sea with

dry feet. Who bade the four spirits of the tempest, which have the power to trouble land and sea, north and south, and west and east, vex neither sea nor land nor the trees that grow on it? Truly these things were ordered by Him who kept this woman safe from the tempest, as well when she awoke as when she slept. But whence might this woman have meat and drink, and how could her sustenance last out to her for three years and more? Who, then, fed Saint Mary the Egyptian in the cavern or in the desert? Assuredly no one but Christ. It was a great miracle to feed five thousand folk with five loaves and two fishes; but God in their great need sent to them abundance."

As to the sentiments and opinions of Chaucer, then, on matters such as these, we can entertain no reasonable doubt. But we are altogether too ill acquainted with the details of his personal life, and with the motives which contributed to determine its course, to be able to arrive at any valid conclusions as to the way in which his principles affected his conduct. Enough has been already said concerning the attitude seemingly observed by him towards the great public questions, and the great historical events, of his day. If he had strong political opinions of his own, or strong personal views on questions either of ecclesiastical policy or of religious doctrine—in which assumptions there seems nothing probable—he, at all events, did not wear his heart on his sleeve, or use his poetry, allegorical or otherwise, as a vehicle of his wishes, hopes, or fears on these heads. The true breath of freedom could hardly be expected to blow through the precincts of a Plantagenet court. If Chaucer could write the pretty lines in the *Manciple's Tale* about the caged bird and its uncontrollable desire for liberty, his contemporary Barbour could

apostrophise Freedom itself as a noble thing, in words
the simple manliness of which stirs the blood after a very
different fashion.   Concerning his domestic relations, we
may regard it as virtually certain that he was unhappy as
a husband, though tender and affectionate as a father.
Considering how vast a proportion of the satire of all
times—but more especially that of the Middle Ages, and
in these again pre-eminently of the period of European
literature which took its tone from Jean de Meung—is directed against woman and against married life, it would be
difficult to decide how much of the irony, sarcasm, and fun
lavished by Chaucer on these themes is due to a fashion
with which he readily fell in, and how much to the impulse of personal feeling.   A perfect anthology, or perhaps one should rather say, a complete herbarium, might
be collected from his works of samples of these attacks on
women.   He has manifestly made a careful study of their
ways, with which he now and then betrays that curiously
intimate acquaintance to which we are accustomed in a
Richardson or a Balzac.   How accurate are such incidental
remarks as this, that women are " full measurable " in such
matters as sleep — not caring for so much of it at a time
as men do !   How wonderfully natural is the description of
Cressid's bevy of lady-visitors, attracted by the news that
she is shortly to be surrendered to the Greeks, and of the
" nice vanity "—*i. e.*, foolish emptiness — of their consola-
tory gossip.   "As men see in town, and all about, that
women are accustomed to visit their friends," so a swarm
of ladies came to Cressid, " and sat themselves down, and
said as I shall tell. ' I am delighted,' says one, ' that you
will so soon see your father.' ' Indeed I am not so delighted,' says another, ' for we have not seen half enough
of her since she has been at Troy.' ' I do hope,' quoth

the third, 'that she will bring us back peace with her; in
which case may Almighty God guide her on her departure.'
And Cressid heard these words and womanish things as if
she were far away; for she was burning all the time with
another passion than any of which they knew; so that she
almost felt her heart die for woe, and for weariness of that
company." But his satire against women is rarely so in-
nocent as this; and though several ladies take part in the
Canterbury Pilgrimage, yet pilgrim after pilgrim has his
saw or jest against their sex. The courteous *Knight* cannot refrain from the generalisation that women all follow
the favour of fortune. The *Summoner*, who is of a less
scrupulous sort, introduces a diatribe against women's passionate love of vengeance; and the *Shipman* seasons a
story which requires no such addition by an enumeration
of their favourite foibles. But the climax is reached in
the confessions of the *Wife of Bath*, who quite unhesitat-
ingly says that women are best won by flattery and busy
attentions; that when won they desire to have the sover-
eignty over their husbands, and that they tell untruths and
swear to them with twice the boldness of men; while as
to the power of their tongue, she quotes the second-hand
authority of her fifth husband for the saying that it is better to dwell with a lion or a foul dragon than with a woman accustomed to chide. It is true that this same *Wife of
Bath* also observes with an effective *tu quoque :*—

> "By God, if women had but written stories,
>   As clerkës have within their oratòries,
>   They would have writ of men more wickednéss
>   Than all the race of Adam may redress ;"

and the *Legend of Good Women* seems, in point of fact,
to have been intended to offer some such kind of amends

as is here declared to be called for.   But the balance still
remains heavy against the poet's sentiments of gallantry
and respect for women.   It should, at the same time, be
remembered that among the *Canterbury Tales* the two
which are of their kind the most effective constitute trib-
utes to the most distinctively feminine and wifely virtue
of fidelity.   Moreover, when coming from such personages
as the pilgrims who narrate the *Tales* in question, the
praise of women has special significance and value.   The
Merchant and the *Shipman* may indulge in facetious or
coarse jibes against wives and their behaviour; but the
Man of Law, full of grave experience of the world, is a
witness above suspicion to the womanly virtue of which
his narrative celebrates so illustrious an example, while the
Clerk of Oxford has in his cloistered solitude, where all
womanly blandishments are unknown, come to the conclusion that

> " Men speak of Job, most for his humbleness,
> As clerkës, when they list, can well indite,
> Of men in special; but, in truthfulness,
> Though praise by clerks of women be but slight,
> No man in humbleness can him acquit
> As women can, nor can be half so true
> As women are, unless all things be new."

As to marriage, Chaucer may be said generally to treat it
in that style of laughing with a wry mouth, which has
from time immemorial been affected both in comic writing
and on the comic stage, but which in the end even the
most determined old bachelor feels an occasional inclination to consider monotonous.

In all this, however, it is obvious that something at least
must be set down to conventionality.   Yet the best part
of Chaucer's nature, it is hardly necessary to say, was

156 CHAUCER. [CHAP.

neither conventional nor commonplace. He was not, we may rest assured, one of that numerous class which in his days, as it does in ours, composed the population of the land of Philistia—the persons so well defined by the Scottish poet, Sir David Lyndsay (himself a courtier of the noblest type):—

> "Who fixèd have their hearts and whole intents
> On sensual lust, on dignity, and rents."

Doubtless Chaucer was a man of practical good sense, desirous of suitable employment and of a sufficient income; nor can we suppose him to have been one of those who look upon social life and its enjoyments with a jaundiced eye, or who, absorbed in things which are not of this world, avert their gaze from it altogether. But it is hardly possible that rank and position should have been valued on their own account by one who so repeatedly recurs to his ideal of the true gentleman, as to a conception dissociated from mere outward circumstances, and more particularly independent of birth or inherited wealth. At times, we know, men find what they seek; and so Chaucer found in Boëthius and in Guillaume de Lorris that conception which he both translates and reproduces, besides repeating it in a little *Ballade*, probably written by him in the last *decennium* of his life. By far the best-known and the finest of these passages is that in the *Wife of Bath's Tale*, which follows the round assertion that the "arrogance" against which it protests is not worth a hen; and which is followed by an appeal to a parallel passage in Dante:—

> "Look, who that is most virtuous alway
> Privy and open, and most intendeth aye

> To do the gentle deedës that he can,
> Take him for the greatest gentleman.
> Christ wills we claim of Him our gentleness,
> Not of our elders for their old richés.
> For though they give us all their heritáge
> Through which we claim to be of high paráge,
> Yet may they not bequeathë for no thing—
> To none of us—their virtuous living,
> That made them gentlemen y-callèd be,
> And bade us follow them in such degree.
> Well can the wisë poet of Florénce,
> That Dante hightë, speak of this senténce;
> Lo, in such manner of rhyme is Dante's tale:
> 'Seldom upriseth by its branches small
> Prowess of man; for God of His prowéss
> Wills that we claim of Him our gentleness;
> For of our ancestors we no thing claim
> But temporal thing, that men may hurt and maim.'"[1]

By the still ignobler greed of money for its own sake, there is no reason whatever to suppose Chaucer to have been at any time actuated; although, under the pressure of immediate want, he devoted a *Complaint* to his empty purse, and made known, in the proper quarters, his desire to see it refilled. Finally, as to what is commonly called pleasure, he may have shared the fashions and even the vices of his age; but we know hardly anything on the subject,

---

[1] The passage in Canto viii. of the *Purgatorio* is thus translated by Longfellow:

> "Not oftentimes upriseth through the branches
> The probity of man; and this He wills
> Who gives it, so that we may ask of Him."

Its intention is only to show that the son is not necessarily what the father is before him; thus, Edward I. of England is a mightier man than was his father Henry III. Chaucer has ingeniously, though not altogether legitimately, pressed the passage into his service.

except that excess in wine, which is often held a pardon-
able peccadillo in a poet, receives his emphatic condemna-
tion. It would be hazardous to assert of him, as Herrick
asserted of himself, that though his " Muse was jocund,
his life was chaste ;" inasmuch as his name occurs in one
unfortunate connexion full of suspiciousness. But we may
at least believe him to have spoken his own sentiments in
the Doctor of Physic's manly declaration that

> " . . . Of all treason sovereign pestilence
> Is when a man betrayeth innocence."

His true pleasures lay far away from those of vanity and
dissipation. In the first place, he seems to have been a
passionate reader. To his love of books he is constantly
referring; indeed, this may be said to be the only kind of
egotism which he seems to. take a pleasure in indulging.
At the opening of his earliest extant poem of consequence,
the *Book of the Duchess,* he tells us how he preferred to
drive away a night rendered sleepless through melancholy
thoughts, by means of a book, which he thought better
entertainment than a game either at chess or at "tables."
This passion lasted longer with him than the other passion
which it had helped to allay ; for in the sequel to the well-
known passage in the *House of Fame,* already cited, he
gives us a glimpse of himself at home, absorbed in his favourite pursuit :—

> " Thou go'st home to thy house anon,
>   And there, as dumb as any stone,
>   Thou sittest at another book,
>   Till fully dazèd is thy look ;
>   And liv'st thus as a hermit quite,
>   Although thy abstinence is slight."

And doubtless he counted the days lost in which he was

prevented from following the rule of life which elsewhere he sets himself, "to study and to read alway, day by day," and pressed even the nights into his service when he was not making his head ache with writing. How eager and, considering the times in which he lived, how diverse a reader he was, has already been abundantly illustrated in the course of this volume. His knowledge of Holy Writ was considerable, though it probably, for the most part, came to him at second-hand. He seems to have had some acquaintance with patristic and homiletic literature; he produced a version of the homily on Mary Magdalene, improperly attributed to Origen; and, as we have seen, emulated King Alfred in translating Boëthius's famous manual of moral philosophy. His Latin learning extended over a wide range of literature, from Virgil and Ovid down to some of the favourite Latin poets of the Middle Ages. It is to be feared that he occasionally read Latin authors with so eager a desire to arrive at the contents of their books that he at times mistook their meaning—not far otherwise, slightly to vary a happy comparison made by one of his most eminent commentators, than many people read Chaucer's own writings now-a-days. That he possessed any knowledge at all of Greek may be doubted, both on general grounds and on account of a little slip or two in quotation of a kind not unusual with those who quote what they have not previously read. His *Troilus and Cressid* has only a very distant connexion, indeed, with Homer, whose *Iliad*, before it furnished materials for the mediæval Troilus-legend, had been filtered through a brief Latin epitome, and diluted into a Latin novel, and a journal kept at the seat of war, of altogether apocryphal value. And, indeed, it must in general be conceded that, if Chaucer had read much, he lays claim to having read more;

for he not only occasionally ascribes to known authors
works which we can by no means feel certain as to their
having written, but at times he even cites (or is made to
cite, in all the editions of his works) authors who are altogether unknown to fame by the names which he gives to
them.   But then it must be remembered that other mediæval writers have rendered themselves liable to the same
kind of charge.   Quoting was one of the dominant literary fashions of the age; and just as a word without an
oath went for but little in conversation, so a statement or
sentiment in writing acquired a greatly enhanced value
when suggested by authority, even after no more precise
a fashion than the use of the phrase "as old books say."
In Chaucer's days the equivalent of the modern "I have
seen it said *somewhere*"—with, perhaps, the venturesome
addition: "I *think*, in Horace"—had clearly not become
an objectionable expletive.

Of modern literatures there can be no doubt that Chaucer had made substantially his own the two which could
be of importance to him as a poet.   His obligations to
the French singers have probably been over-estimated—at
all events, if the view adopted in this essay be the correct
one, and if the charming poem of the *Flower and the Leaf*,
together with the lively, but as to its meaning not very
transparent, so-called *Chaucer's Dream*, be denied admission among his genuine works.   At the same time, the influence of the *Roman de la Rose* and that of the courtly
poets, of whom Machault was the chief in France and
Froissart the representative in England, are perceptible in
Chaucer almost to the last, nor is it likely that he should
ever have ceased to study and assimilate them.   On the
other hand, the extent of his knowledge of Italian literature has probably till of late been underrated in an almost

equal degree.   This knowledge displays itself not only in
the imitation or adaptation of particular poems, but more
especially in the use made of incidental passages and details.   In this way his debts to Dante were especially numerous ; and it is curious to find proofs so abundant of
Chaucer's relatively close study of a poet with whose genius his own had so few points in common.   Notwithstanding first appearances, it is an open question whether Chaucer had ever read Boccaccio's *Decamerone*, with which he
may merely have had in common the sources of several
of his *Canterbury Tales*.   But as he certainly took one
of them from the *Teseide* (without improving it in the
process), and not less certainly, and adapted the *Filostrato*
in his *Troilus and Cressid*, it is strange that he should refrain from naming the author to whom he was more in-
debted than to any one other for poetic materials.

But wide and diverse as Chaucer's reading fairly de-
serves to be called, the love of nature was even stronger
and more absorbing in him than the love of books.   He
has himself, in a very charming passage, compared the
strength of the one and of the other of his predilections :—

> " And as for me, though I have knowledge slight,
>   In bookës for to read I me delight,
>   And to them give I faith and full credénce,
>   And in my heart have them in reverence
>   So heartily, that there is gamë none
>   That from my bookës maketh me be gone,
>   But it be seldom on the holiday—
>   Save, certainly, when that the month of May
>   Is come, and that I hear the fowlës sing,
>   And see the flowers as they begin to spring,
>   Farewell my book, and my devotión."

Undoubtedly the literary fashion of Chaucer's times is

8

responsible for part of this May-morning sentiment, with
which he is fond of beginning his poems (the Canterbury
pilgrimage is dated towards the end of April—but is not
April "messenger to May?"). It had been decreed that
flowers should be the badges of nations and dynasties,
and the tokens of amorous sentiment; the rose had its
votaries, and the lily, lauded by Chaucer's *Prioress* as
the symbol of the Blessed Virgin; while the daisy, which
first sprang from the tears of a forlorn damsel, in France
gave its name (*marguérite*) to an entire species of courtly
verse. The enthusiastic adoration professed by Chaucer,
in the *Prologue* to the *Legend of Good Women*, for the
daisy, which he afterwards identifies with the good Alceste, the type of faithful wifehood, is, of course, a mere
poetical figure. But there is in his use of these favourite
literary devices, so to speak, a variety in sameness significant of their accordance with his own taste, and of the
frank and fresh love of nature which animated him, and
which seems to us as much a part of him as his love of
books. It is unlikely that his personality will ever become more fully known than it is at present; nor is there
anything in respect of which we seem to see so clearly
into his inner nature as with regard to these twin predilections, to which he remains true in all his works and in
all his moods. While the study of books was his chief
passion, nature was his chief joy and solace; while his
genius enabled him to transfuse what he read in the former, what came home to him in the latter was akin to that
genius itself; for he at times reminds us of his own fresh
Canace, whom he describes as looking so full of happiness
during her walk through the wood at sunrise:—

> "What for the season, what for the morning
> And for the fowlës that she heardë sing,

> For right anon she wistë what they meant
> Right by their song, and knew all their intent."

If the above view of Chaucer's character and intellectual tastes and tendencies be in the main correct, there will
seem to be nothing paradoxical in describing his literary
progress, so far as its *data* are ascertainable, as a most steady
and regular one.　Very few men awake to find themselves
either famous or great of a sudden, and perhaps as few poets
as other men, though it may be heresy against a venerable
maxim to say so.　Chaucer's works form a clearly recognisable series of steps towards the highest achievement
of which, under the circumstances in which he lived and
wrote, he can be held to have been capable; and his long
and arduous self-training, whether consciously or not directed to a particular end, was of that sure kind from which
genius itself derives strength.　His beginnings as a writer
were dictated, partly by the impulse of that imitative
faculty which, in poetic natures, is the usual precursor of
the creative, partly by the influence of prevailing tastes
and the absence of native English literary predecessors
whom, considering the circumstances of his life and the
nature of his temperament, he could have found it a congenial task to follow.　French poems were, accordingly, his
earliest models; but fortunately (unlike Gower, whom it is
so instructive to compare with Chaucer, precisely because
the one lacked that gift of genius which the other possessed) he seems at once to have resolved to make use for his
poetical writings of his native speech.　In no way, therefore, could he have begun his career with so happy a promise of its future as in that which he actually chose.　Nor
could any course so naturally have led him to introduce
into his poetic diction the French idioms and words already used in the spoken language of Englishmen, more

especially in those classes for which he in the first instance wrote, and thus to confer upon our tongue the great benefit which it owes to him. Again, most fortunately, others had already pointed the way to the selection for literary use of that English dialect which was probably the most suitable for the purpose ; and Chaucer, as a Southern man (like his *Parson of a Town*), belonged to a part of the country where the old alliterative verse had long since been discarded for classical and romance forms of versification. Thus the *Romaunt of the Rose* most suitably opens his literary life — a translation in which there is nothing original except an occasional turn of phrase, but in which the translator finds opportunity for exercising his powers of judgment by virtually re-editing the work before him. And already in the *Book of the Duchess*, though most unmistakeably a follower of Machault, he is also the rival of the great French *trouvère*, and has advanced in freedom of movement not less than in agreeableness of form. Then, as his travels extended his acquaintance with foreign literatures to that of Italy, he here found abundant fresh materials from which to feed his productive powers, and more elaborate forms in which to clothe their results ; while at the same time comparison, the kindly nurse of originality, more and more enabled him to recast instead of imitating, or encouraged him freely to invent. In *Troilus and Cressid* he produced something very different from a mere condensed translation, and achieved a work in which he showed himself a master of poetic expression and sustained narrative ; in the *House of Fame* and the *Assembly of Fowls* he moved with freedom in happily contrived allegories of his own invention ; and with the *Legend of Good Women* he had already arrived at a stage when he could undertake to review, under a pleasant pretext, but with evident consciousness of work done, the list of his previous works. "He hath," he said of himself, "made many a lay and many a thing." Meanwhile the labour incidentally devoted by him to translation from the Latin, or to the composition of prose treatises in the scholastic manner of academical exercises, could but little affect his general literary progress. The mere scholarship of youth, even if it be the reverse of close and profound, is wont to cling to a man through life, and to assert its modest claims at any season; and thus Chaucer's school-learning exercised little influence either of an advancing or of a retarding kind upon the full development of his genius. Nowhere is he so truly himself as in the masterpiece of his last years. For the *Canterbury Tales*, in which he is at once greatest, most original, and most catholic in the choice of materials as well as in moral sympathies, bears the unmistakeable stamp of having formed the crowning labour of his life—a work which death alone prevented him from completing.

It may be said, without presumption, that such a general view as this leaves ample room for all reasonable theories as to the chronology and sequence, where these remain more or less unsettled, of Chaucer's indisputably genuine works. In any case, there is no poet whom, if only as an exercise in critical analysis, it is more interesting to study and re-study in connexion with the circumstances of his literary progress. He still, as has been seen, belongs to the Middle Ages, but to a period in which the noblest ideals of these Middle Ages are already beginning to pale and their mightiest institutions to quake around him; in which learning continues to be in the main scholasticism, the linking of argument with argument, and the accumulation of authority upon authority, and poetry remains to a great extent the crabbedness of clerks or the formality

of courts. Again, Chaucer is mediæval in tricks of style
and turns of phrase ; he often contents himself with the
tritest of figures and the most unrefreshing of ancient devices, and freely resorts to a mixture of names and associations belonging to his own times with others derived
from other ages. This want of literary perspective is a
sure sign of mediævalism, and one which has amused the
world, or has jarred upon it, since the Renascence taught
men to study both classical and Biblical antiquity as reali-
ties, and not merely as a succession of pictures or of tap-
estries on a wall. Chaucer mingles things mediæval and
things classical as freely as he brackets King David with
the philosopher Seneca, or Judas Iscariot with the Greek
"dissimulator" Sinon.   His Dido, mounted on a stout
palfrey paper-white of hue, with a red-and-gold saddle
embroidered and embossed, resembles Alice Perrers in all
her pomp rather than the Virgilian queen. Jupiter's eagle, the poet's guide and instructor in the allegory of the
House of Fame, invokes "Saint Mary, Saint James," and
"Saint Clare" all at once ; and the pair of lovers at Troy
sign their letters "*la vostre T*." and "*la vostre C*." An-
achronisms of this kind (of the danger of which, by the
way, to judge from a passage in the *Prologue* to the *Legend
of Good Women*, Chaucer would not appear to have been
wholly unconscious) are intrinsically of very slight importance. But the morality of Chaucer's narratives is at
times the artificial and overstrained morality of the Middle
Ages, which, as it were, clutches hold of a single idea to
the exclusion of all others—a morality which, when carried to its extreme consequences, makes monomaniacs as
well as martyrs, in both of which species, occasionally,
perhaps, combined in the same persons, the Middle Ages
abound.   The fidelity of Griseldis under the trials imposed

upon her by her, in point of fact, brutal husband is the fidelity of a martyr to unreason. The story was afterwards put on the stage in the Elizabethan age; and though even in the play of *Patient Grissil* (by Chettle and others) it is not easy to reconcile the husband's proceedings with the promptings of common sense, yet the playwrights, with the instinct of their craft, contrived to introduce some element of humanity into his character, and of probability into his conduct. Again, the supra-chivalrous respect paid by Arviragus, the Breton knight of the *Franklin's Tale*, to the sanctity of his wife's word, seriously to the peril of his own and his wife's honour, is an effort to which probably even the Knight of La Mancha himself would have proved unequal. It is not to be expected that Chaucer should have failed to share some of the prejudices of his times as well as to fall in with their ways of thought and sentiment; and though it is the *Prioress* who tells a story against the Jews which passes the legend of Hugh of Lincoln, yet it would be very hazardous to seek any irony in this legend of bigotry. In general, much of that *naïveté* which to modern readers seems Chaucer's most obvious literary quality must be ascribed to the times in which he lived and wrote. This quality is, in truth, by no means that which most deeply impresses itself upon the observation of any one able to compare Chaucer's writings with those of his more immediate predecessors and successors. But the sense in which the term *naïf* should be understood in literary criticism is so imperfectly agreed upon among us, that we have not yet even found an English equivalent for the word.

To Chaucer's times, then, belongs much of what may at first sight seem to include itself among the characteristics of his genius; while, on the other hand, there are to be

distinguished from these the influences due to his training
and studies in two literatures—the French and the Italian.
In the former of these he must have felt at home, if not
by birth and descent, at all events by social connexion,
habits of life, and ways of thought; while in the latter he,
whose own country's was still a half-fledged literary life,
found ready to his hand masterpieces of artistic maturity
lofty in conception, broad in bearing, finished in form.
There still remain, for summary review, the elements proper to his own poetic individuality—those which mark him
out not only as the first great poet of his own nation, but
as a great poet for all times.

The poet must please; if he wishes to be successful and
popular, he must suit himself to the tastes of his public;
and even if he be indifferent to immediate fame, he must,
as belonging to one of the most impressionable, the most
receptive species of humankind, live, in a sense, *with* and
for his generation. To meet this demand upon his genius, Chaucer was born with many gifts which he carefully
and assiduously exercised in a long series of poetical ex-
periments, and which he was able felicitously to combine
for the achievement of results unprecedented in our literature. In readiness of descriptive power, in brightness
and variety of imagery, and in flow of diction, Chaucer
remained unequalled by any English poet, till he was sur-
passed—it seems not too much to say, in all three respects
—by Spenser. His verse, where it suits his purpose, glit-
ters, to use Dunbar's expression, as with fresh enamel, and
its hues are variegated like those of a Flemish tapestry.
Even where his descriptive enumerations seem at first sight
monotonous or perfunctory, they are, in truth, graphic and
true in their details, as in the list of birds in the *Assembly
of Fowls*, quoted in part on an earlier page of this essay,

and in the shorter list of trees in the same poem, which
is, however, in its general features, imitated from Boccaccio. Neither King James I. of Scotland, nor Spenser,
who after Chaucer essayed similar *tours de force*, were
happier than he had been before them. Or we may refer
to the description of the preparations for the tournament
and of the tournament itself in the *Knight's Tale*, or to the
thoroughly Dutch picture of a disturbance in a farm-yard
in the *Nun's Priest's*. The vividness with which Chaucer
describes scenes and events as if he had them before his
own eyes, was no doubt, in the first instance, a result of
his own imaginative temperament; but one would probably not go wrong in attributing the fulness of the use
which he made of this gift to the influence of his Italian
studies—more especially to those which led him to Dante,
whose multitudinous characters and scenes impress themselves with so singular and immediate a definiteness upon
the imagination. At the same time, Chaucer's resources
seem inexhaustible for filling up or rounding off his narratives with the aid of chivalrous love or religious legend,
by the introduction of samples of scholastic discourse or
devices of personal or general allegory. He commands,
where necessary, a rhetorician's readiness of illustration,
and a masque-writer's inventiveness, as to machinery; he
can even (in the *House of Fame*) conjure up an elaborate
but self-consistent phantasmagory of his own, and continue
it with a fulness proving that his fancy would not be at
a loss for supplying even more materials than he cares to
employ.

But Chaucer's poetry derived its power to please from
yet another quality; and in this he was the first of our
English poets to emulate the poets of the two literatures
to which, in the matter of his productions and in the or-

8*

naments of his diction, he owed so much. There is in
his verse a music which hardly ever wholly loses itself,
and which at times is as sweet as that in any English
poet after him.

This assertion is not one which is likely to be gainsaid
at the present day, when there is not a single lover of
Chaucer who would sit down contented with Dryden's
condescending mixture of censure and praise. "The verse
of Chaucer," he wrote, "I confess, is not harmonious to
us. They who lived with him, and some time after him,
thought it musical; and it continues so, even in our judgment, if compared with the numbers of Lydgate and Gower, his contemporaries: there is a rude sweetness of a
Scotch tune in it, which is natural and pleasing, though
not perfect." At the same time, it is no doubt necessary,
in order to verify the correctness of a less balanced judgment, to take the trouble, which, if it could but be be-
lieved, is by no means great, to master the rules and
usages of Chaucerian versification. These rules and usages
the present is not a fit occasion for seeking to explain.[1]

[1] It may, however, be stated that they only partially connect themselves with Chaucer's use of forms which are now obsolete—more
especially of inflexions of verbs and substantives (including several
instances of the famous final _e_), and contractions with the negative
_ne_ and other monosyllabic words ending in a vowel, of the initial syllables of words beginning with vowels or with the letter _h_. These
and other variations from later usage in spelling and pronunciation
—such as the occurrence of an _e_ (sometimes sounded and sometimes
not) at the end of words in which it is now no longer retained, and,
again, the frequent accentuation of many words of French origin in
their last syllable, as in French, and of certain words of English origin analogously—are to be looked for as a matter of course in a last
writing in the period of our language in which Chaucer lived. He
clearly foresaw the difficulties which would be caused to his readers
by the variations of usage in spelling and pronunciation—variations

With regard to the most important of them, is it not
too much to say that instinct and experience will very

to some extent rendered inevitable by the fact that he wrote in an
English dialect which was only gradually coming to be accepted as
the uniform language of English writers. Towards the close of his
Troilus and Cressid he thus addresses his "little book," in fear of
the mangling it might undergo from scriveners who might blunder
in the copying of its words, or from reciters who might maltreat its
verse in the distribution of the accents:—

> "And, since there is so great diversity
>   In English, and in writing of our tongue,
>   I pray to God that none may míswrite thee
>   Nor thee mismetre, for default of tongue,
>   And wheresoe'er thou mayst be read or sung,
>   That thou be understood, God I beseech."

But in his versification he likewise adopted certain other practices
which had no such origin or reason as those already referred to.
Among them were the addition, at the end of a line of five accents,
of an unaccented syllable; and the substitution, for the first foot of
a line either of four or of five accents, of a single syllable. These
deviations from a stricter system of versification he doubtless permitted to himself, partly for the sake of variety, and partly for that
of convenience; but neither of them is peculiar to himself, or of supreme importance for the effect of his verse. In fact, he seems to
allow as much in a passage of his *House of Fame*—a poem written, it
should, however, be observed, in an easy-going form of verse (the line
of four accents) which in his later period Chaucer seems, with this
exception, to have invariably discarded. He here beseeches Apollo
to make his rhyme

> ". . . Somewhat agreeáble,
>   Though some verse fail in a sylláble."

But another of his usages—the misunderstanding of which has more
than anything else caused his art as a writer of verse to be misjudged
—seems to have been due to a very different cause. To understand
the real nature of the usage in question it is only necessary to seize
the principle of Chaucer's rhythm. Of this principle it was well said
many years ago by a most competent authority—Mr. R. Horne—that

speedily combine to indicate to an intelligent reader where
the poet has resorted to it. *Without* intelligence on the
part of the reader, the beautiful harmonies of Mr. Tenny-
son's later verse remain obscure; so that, taken in this
way, the most musical of English verse may seem as difficult to read as the most rugged; but in the former case
the lesson is learnt not to be lost again; in the latter, the
tumbling is ever beginning anew, as with the rock of
Sisyphus.   There is nothing that can fairly be called rugged in the verse of Chaucer.

And, fortunately, there are not many pages in this poet's
works devoid of lines or passages the music of which cannot escape any ear, however unaccustomed it may be to
his diction and versification.   What is the nature of the
art at whose bidding ten monosyllables arrange themselves
into a line of the exquisite cadence of the following :—

> "And she was fair, as is the rose in May?"

Nor would it be easy to find lines surpassing in their melancholy charm Chaucer's version of the lament of Medea
when deserted by Jason—a passage which makes the reader

---

it is "inseparable from a full or fair exercise of the genius of our
language in versification."   For though this usage in its full freedom
was gradually again lost to our poetry for a time, yet it was in a large
measure recovered by Shakspeare and the later dramatists of our
great age, and has since been never altogether abandoned again—not
even by the correct writers of the Augustan period—till by the favourites of our own times it is resorted to with a perhaps excessive
liberality.   It consists simply in *slurring* over certain final syllables
—not eliding them or contracting them with the syllables following
upon them, but passing over them lightly, so that, without being in-
audible, they may at the same time not interfere with the rhythm or
beat of the verse.   This usage, by adding to the variety, incontestably
adds to the flexibility and beauty of Chaucer's versification.

neglectful of the English poet's modest hint that the letter
of the Colchian princess may be found at full length in
Ovid.　The lines shall be quoted *verbatim*, though not
literatim ; and perhaps no better example, and none more
readily appreciable by a modern ear, could be given than
the fourth of them of the harmonious effect of Chaucer's
usage of *slurring*, referred to above :—

> " Why likèd thee my yellow hair to see
> More than the boundës of mine honesty?
> Why likèd me thy youth and thy fairnéss
> And of thy tongue the infinite graciousness?
> O, had'st thou in thy conquest dead y-bee(n),
> Full myckle untruth had there died with thee."

Qualities and powers such as the above have belonged
to poets of very various times and countries before and
after Chaucer.　But in addition to these he most assuredly
possessed others, which are not usual among the poets of
our nation, and which, whencesoever they had come to him
personally, had not, before they made their appearance in
him, seemed indigenous to the English soil.　It would, indeed, be easy to misrepresent the history of English poetry,
during the period which Chaucer's advent may be said to
have closed, by ascribing to it a uniformly solemn and
serious, or even dark and gloomy, character.　Such a description would not apply to the poetry of the period before the Norman Conquest, though, in truth, little room
could be left for the play of fancy or wit in the hammer-
ed-out war-song, or in the long-drawn Scriptural paraphrase.
Nor was it likely that a contagious gaiety should find an
opportunity of manifesting itself in the course of the versification of grave historical chronicles, or in the tranquil
objective reproduction of the endless traditions of British
legend.　Of the popular songs belonging to the period

after the Norman Conquest, the remains which furnish us
with direct or indirect evidence concerning them hardly
enable us to form an opinion. But we know that (the
cavilling spirit of Chaucer's burlesque *Rhyme of Sir
Thopas* notwithstanding) the efforts of English metrical
romance in the thirteenth and fourteenth centuries were
neither few nor feeble, although these romances were chiefly translations, sometimes abridgments to boot—even the
Arthurian cycle having been only imported across the
Channel, though it may have thus come back to its original
home. There is some animation in at least one famous
chronicle in verse, dating from about the close of the thirteenth century; there is real spirit in the war-songs of
Minot in the middle of the fourteenth; and from about
its beginnings dates a satire full of broad fun concerning
the jolly life led by the monks. But none of these works
or of those contemporary with them show that innate lightness and buoyancy of tone which seems to add wings to
the art of poetry. Nowhere had the English mind found
so real an opportunity of poetic utterance in the days of
Chaucer's own youth as in Langland's unique work, national in its allegorical form and in its alliterative metre; and nowhere had this utterance been more stern and
severe.

No sooner, however, has Chaucer made his appearance
as a poet, than he seems to show what mistress's badge he
wears, which party of the two that have at most times
divided among them a national literature and its representatives he intends to follow. The burden of his song is
"Si douce est la marguérite:" he has learnt the ways of
French gallantry as if to the manner born, and thus becomes, as it were without hesitation or effort, the first
English love-poet. Nor—though in the course of his

career his range of themes, his command of materials, and his choice of forms are widely enlarged—is the gay banner under which he has ranged himself ever deserted by him. With the exception of the *House of Fame,* there is not one of his longer poems of which the passion of love, under one or another of its aspects, does not either constitute the main subject or (as in the *Canterbury Tales*) furnish the greater part of the contents. It is as a love-poet that Gower thinks of Chaucer when paying a tribute to him in his own verse; it is to the attacks made upon him in his character as a love-poet, and to his consciousness of what he has achieved as such, that he gives expression in the *Prologue* to the *Legend of Good Women,* where his fair advocate tells the God of Love :—

> "The man hath servèd you of his cunníng,
> And furthered well your law in his writíng,
> All be it that he cannot well indite,
> Yet hath he made unlearnèd folk delight
> To servë you in praising of your name."

And so he resumes his favourite theme once more, to tell, as the *Man of Law* says, "of lovers up and down, more than Ovid makes mention of in his old *Epistles.*" This fact alone—that our first great English poet was also our first English love-poet, properly so called—would have sufficed to transform our poetic literature through his agency.

What, however, calls for special notice, in connexion with Chaucer's special poetic quality of gaiety and brightness, is the preference which he exhibits for treating the joyous aspects of this many-sided passion. Apart from the *Legend of Good Women,* which is specially designed to give brilliant examples of the faithfulness of women under circumstances of trial, pain, and grief, and from two or

three of the *Canterbury Tales*, he dwells, with consistent
preference, on the bright side of love, though remaining a
stranger to its divine radiance, which shines forth so fully
upon us out of the pages of Spenser. Thus, in the *Assembly of Fowls* all is gaiety and mirth, as indeed beseems
the genial neighbourhood of Cupid's temple. Again, in
Troilus and Cressid, the earlier and cheerful part of the
love-story is that which he develops with unmistakeable
sympathy and enjoyment; and in his hands this part of
the poem becomes one of the most charming poetic narratives of the birth and growth of young love which our
literature possesses—a soft and sweet counterpart to the
consuming heat of Marlowe's unrivalled *Hero and Leander*.
With Troilus it was love at first sight—with Cressid a
passion of very gradual growth. But so full of nature is
the narrative of this growth, that one is irresistibly reminded at more than one point of the inimitable creations
of the great modern master in the description of women's
love. Is there not a touch of Gretchen in Cressid, retir-
ing into her chamber to ponder over the first revelation to
her of the love of Troilus ?—

> " Cressid arose, no longer there she stayed,
>   But straight into her closet went anon,
>   And set her down, as still as any stone,
>   And every word gan up and down to wind,
>   That he had said, as it came to her mind."

And is there not a touch of Clärchen in her—though with
a difference—when from her casement she blushingly be-
holds her lover riding past in triumph :

> " So like a man of armës and a knight
>   He was to see, filled full of high prowéss,
>   For both he had a body, and a might

To do that thing, as well as hardiness;
And eke to see him in his gear him dress,
So fresh, so young, so wieldly seemèd he,
It truly was a heaven him for to see.

" His helm was hewn about in twenty places,
That by a tissue hung his back behind;
His shield was dashed with strokes of swords and maces,
In which men mightë many an arrow find
That piercèd had the horn and nerve and rind;
And aye the people cried: 'Here comes our joy,
And, next his brother, holder up of Troy.' "

Even in the very *Book of the Duchess*, the widowed lover
describes the maiden charms of his lost wife with so lively
a freshness as almost to make one forget that it is a *lost*
wife whose praises are being recorded.

The vivacity and joyousness of Chaucer's poetic temperament, however, show themselves in various other ways besides his favourite manner of treating a favourite theme.
They enhance the spirit of his passages of dialogue, and
add force and freshness to his passages of description.
They make him amusingly impatient of epical lengths,
abrupt in his transitions, and anxious, with an anxiety usually manifested by readers rather than by writers, to come
to the point, " to the great effect," as he is wont to call
it. " Men," he says, " may overlade a ship or barge, and
therefore I will skip at once to the effect, and let all the
rest slip." And he unconsciously suggests a striking difference between himself and the great Elizabethan epic poet
who owes so much to him, when he declines to make as
long a tale of the chaff or of the straw as of the corn, and
to describe all the details of a marriage-feast *seriatim :*

" The fruit of every tale is for to say:
They eat and drink, and dance and sing and play."

This may be the fruit; but epic poets, from Homer downwards, have been generally in the habit of not neglecting the foliage. Spenser, in particular, has that impartial copiousness which we think it our duty to admire in the Ionic epos, but which, if the truth were told, has prevented generations of Englishmen from acquiring an intimate personal acquaintance with the *Fairy Queen*. With Chaucer the danger certainly rather lay in an opposite direction. Most assuredly he can tell a story with admirable point and precision, when he wishes to do so. Perhaps no better example of his skill in this respect could be cited than the *Manciple's Tale*, with its rapid narrative, its major and minor catastrophe, and its concise moral, ending thus:—

> "My son, beware, and be no author new
> Of tidings, whether they be false or true ;
> Whereso thou comest, among high or low,
> Keep well thy tongue, and think upon the crow."

At the same time, his frequently recurring announcements of his desire to be brief have the effect of making his narrative appear to halt, and thus, unfortunately, defeat their own purpose. An example of this may be found in the *Knight's Tale*, a narrative poem of which, in contrast with its beauties, a want of evenness is one of the chief defects. It is not that the desire to suppress redundancies is a tendency deserving anything but commendation in any writer, whether great or small; but rather, that the art of concealing art had not yet dawned upon Chaucer. And yet few writers of any time have taken a more evident pleasure in the process of literary production, and have more visibly overflowed with sympathy for, or antipathy against, the characters of their own creation. Great novelists of our own age have often told their readers, in prefaces to

their fictions or in *quasi*-confidential comments upon them,
of the intimacy in which they have lived with the offspring
of their own brain, to them far from shadowy beings.
But only the *naïveté* of Chaucer's literary age, together
with the vivacity of his manner of thought and writing,
could place him in so close a personal relation towards the
personages and the incidents of his poems. He is overcome by "pity and ruth" as he reads of suffering, and
his eyes "wax foul and sore" as he prepares to tell of its
infliction. He compassionates "love's servants" as if he
were their own "brother dear;" and into his adaptation
of the eventful story of Constance (the *Man of Law's
Tale*) he introduces apostrophe upon apostrophe, to the
defenceless condition of his heroine—to her relentless en-
emy the Sultana, and to Satan, who ever makes his instrument of women "when he will beguile"—to the drunken
messenger who allowed the letter carried by him to be
stolen from him—and to the treacherous Queen-mother
who caused them to be stolen. Indeed, in addressing the
last-named personage, the poet seems to lose all control
over himself.

> "O Domegild, I have no English digne
> Unto thy malice and thy tyranny :
> And therefore to the fiend I thee resign,
> Let him at length tell of thy treachery.
> Fye, mannish, fye !—Oh nay, by God, I lie ;
> Fye fiendish spirit, for I dare well tell,
> Though thou here walk, thy spirit is in hell."

At the opening of the *Legend of Ariadne* he bids Minos
redden with shame ; and towards its close, when narrating
how Theseus sailed away, leaving his true-love behind, he
expresses a hope that the wind may drive the traitor "a
twenty devil way." Nor does this vivacity find a less

amusing expression in so trifling a touch as that in the
Clerk's Tale, where the domestic sent to deprive Griseldis
of her boy becomes, *eo ipso* as it were, " this ugly sergeant."

Closely allied to Chaucer's liveliness and gaiety of disposition, and in part springing from them, are his keen
sense of the ridiculous and the power of satire which he
has at his command. His humour has many varieties,
ranging from the refined and half-melancholy irony of the
House of Fame to the ready wit of the sagacious uncle of
Cressid, the burlesque fun of the inimitable *Nun's Priest's
Tale*, and the very gross salt of the *Reeve*, the *Miller*, and
one or two others. The springs of humour often capri-
ciously refuse to allow themselves to be discovered; nor
is the satire of which the direct intention is transparent
invariably the most effective species of satire. Concerning, however, Chaucer's use of the power which he in so
large a measure possessed, viz., that of covering with ridi-
cule the palpable vices or weaknesses of the classes or
kinds of men represented by some of his character-types,
one assertion may be made with tolerable safety. Whatever may have been the first stimulus and the ultimate scope
of the wit and humour which he here expended, they are
not to be explained as moral indignation in disguise. And
in truth Chaucer's merriment flows spontaneously from a
source very near the surface; he is so extremely diverting,
because he is so extremely diverted himself.

Herein, too, lies the harmlessness of Chaucer's fun. Its
harmlessness, to wit, for those who are able to read him
in something like the spirit in which he wrote—never a
very easy achievement with regard to any author, and one
which the beginner and the young had better be advised
to abstain from attempting with Chaucer in the overflow
of his more or less unrestrained moods. At all events,

the excuse of gaiety of heart—the plea of that *vieil esprit Gaulois* which is so often, and very rarely without need, invoked in an exculpatory capacity by modern French criticism—is the best defence ever made for Chaucer's laughable irregularities, either by his apologists or by himself. "Men should not," he says, and says very truly, "make earnest of game." But when he audaciously defends himself against the charge of impropriety by declaring that he must tell stories *in character*, and coolly requests any person who may find anything in one of his tales objectionable to turn to another:—

> "For he shall find enough, both great and small,
> Of storial thing that toucheth gentleness,
> Likewise morality and holiness;
> Blame ye not me, if ye should choose amiss—"

we are constrained to shake our heads at the transparent sophistry of the plea, which requires no exposure. For Chaucer knew very well how to give life and colour to his page without recklessly disregarding bounds the neglect of which was even in his day offensive to many besides the "*precious* folk" of whom he half derisively pretends to stand in awe. In one instance he defeated his own purpose; for the so-called *Cook's Tale of Gamelyn* was substituted by some earlier editor for the original *Cook's Tale*, which has thus in its completed form become a rarity removed beyond the reach of even the most ardent of curiosity hunters. Fortunately, however, Chaucer spoke the truth when he said that from this point of view he had written very differently at different times; no whiter pages remain than many of his.

But the realism of Chaucer is something more than exuberant love of fun and light-hearted gaiety. He is the first great painter of character, because he is the first great

observer of it among modern European writers. His power of comic observation need not be dwelt upon again,
after the illustrations of it which have been incidentally
furnished in these pages. More especially with regard to
the manners and ways of women, which often, while seeming so natural to women themselves, appear so odd to
male observers, Chaucer's eye was ever on the alert. But
his works likewise contain passages displaying a penetrating insight into the minds of men, as well as a keen eye
for their manners, together with a power of generalising,
which, when kept within due bounds, lies at the root of the
wise knowledge of humankind so admirable to us in our
great essayists, from Bacon to Addison and his modern
successors. How truly, for instance, in *Troilus and Cressid*, Chaucer observes on the enthusiastic belief of converts, the "strongest-faithed" of men, as he understands!
And how fine is the saying as to the suspiciousness characteristic of lewd (*i. e.*, ignorant) people, that to things
which are made more subtly

> "Than they can in their lewdness comprehend,"

they gladly give the worst interpretation which suggests
itself! How appositely the *Canon's Yeoman* describes
the arrogance of those who are too clever by half; "when
a man has an over-great wit," he says, "it very often
chances to him to misuse it!" And with how ripe a wisdom, combined with ethics of true gentleness, the honest
Franklin, at the opening of his *Tale*, discourses on the
uses and the beauty of long-suffering:—

> "For one thing, sirës, safely dare I say,
>   That friends the one the other must obey,
>   If they will longë holdë company.
>   Love will not be constrain'd by mastery.

When mastery comes, the god of love anon
Beateth his wings—and, farewell! he is gone.
Love is a thing as any spirit free.
Women desire, by nature, liberty,
And not to be constrainèd as a thrall;
And so do men, if I the truth say shall.
Look, who that is most patient in love,
He is at his advantage all above.
A virtue high is patience, certain,
Because it vanquisheth, as clerks explain,
Things to which rigour never could attain.
For every word men should not chide and plain;
Learn ye to suffer, or else, so may I go,
Ye shall it learn, whether ye will or no.
For in this world certain no wight there is
Who neither doth nor saith some time amiss.
Sickness or ire, or constellation,
Wine, woe, or changing of complexion,
Causeth full oft to do amiss or speak.
For every wrong men may not vengeance wreak:
After a time there must be temperance
With every wight that knows self-governance."

It was by virtue of his power of observing and drawing
character, above all, that Chaucer became the true predecessor of two several growths in our literature, in both of
which characterisation forms a most important element—
it might perhaps be truly said, the element which surpasses
all others in importance. From this point of view the
dramatic poets of the Elizabethan age remain unequalled
by any other school or group of dramatists, and the English novelists of the eighteenth and nineteenth centuries
by the representatives of any other development of prose-
fiction. In the art of construction, in the invention and
the arrangement of incident, these dramatists and novelists
may have been left behind by others; in the creation of

character they are, on the whole, without rivals in their respective branches of literature.   To the earlier at least of
these growths Chaucer may be said to have pointed the
way.   His personages—more especially, of course, as has
been seen, those who are assembled together in the *Prologue* to the *Canterbury Tales*—are not mere phantasms of
the brain, or even mere actual possibilities, but real human
beings, and types true to the likeness of whole classes of
men and women, or to the mould in which all human nature is cast.   This is, upon the whole, the most wonderful,
as it is perhaps the most generally recognised, of Chaucer's
gifts.   It would not of itself have sufficed to make him a
great dramatist, had the drama stood ready for him as a
literary form into which to pour the inspirations of his
genius, as it afterwards stood ready for our great Eliza-
bethans.   But to it were added in him that perception of
a strong dramatic situation, and that power of finding the
right words for it, which have determined the success of
many plays, and the absence of which materially detracts
from the completeness of the effect of others, high as their
merits may be in other respects.   How thrilling, for instance, is that rapid passage across the stage, as one might
almost call it, of the unhappy Dorigen in the *Franklin's
Tale!*   The antecedents of the situation, to be sure, are,
as has been elsewhere suggested, absurd enough ; but who
can fail to feel that spasm of anxious sympathy with which
a powerful dramatic situation in itself affects us, when the
wife, whom for truth's sake her husband has bidden be
untrue to him, goes forth on her unholy errand of duty ?
" Whither so fast ?" asks the lover :

> "And she made answer, half as she were mad:
> 'Unto the garden, as my husband bade,
> My promise for to keep, alas! alas !'"

Nor, as the abbreviated prose version of the *Pardoner's Tale* given above will suffice to show, was Chaucer deficient in the art of dramatically arranging a story; while he is not excelled by any of our non-dramatic poets in the spirit and movement of his dialogue. The *Book of the Duchess* and the *House of Fame*, but more especially *Troilus and Cressid* and the connecting passages between some of the *Canterbury Tales*, may be referred to in various illustration of this.

The vividness of his imagination, which conjures up, so to speak, the very personality of his characters before him, and the contagious force of his pathos, which is as true and as spontaneous as his humour, complete in him the born dramatist. We can see Constance as with our own eyes, in the agony of her peril:—

> " Have ye not seen some time a pallid face
>   Among a press, of him that hath been led
>   Towards his death, where him awaits no grace,
>   And such a colour in his face hath had,
>   Men mightë know his face was so bested
>   'Mong all the other faces in that rout?
>   So stands Constánce, and looketh her about."

And perhaps there is no better way of studying the general character of Chaucer's pathos than a comparison of the *Monk's Tale* from which this passage is taken, and the *Clerk's Tale*, with their originals. In the former, for instance, the prayer of Constance, when condemned through Domegild's guilt to be cast adrift once more on the waters, her piteous words and tenderness to her little child as it lies weeping in her arm, and her touching leave-taking from the land of the husband who has condemned her—all these are Chaucer's own. So also are parts of one of the most affecting passages in the *Clerk's Tale*—Griseldis'

9

farewell to her daughter. But it is as unnecessary to lay a finger upon lines and passages illustrating Chaucer's pathos as upon others illustrating his humour.

Thus, then, Chaucer was a born dramatist; but fate willed it, that the branch of our literature which might probably have of all been the best suited to his genius was not to spring into life till he and several generations after him had passed away. To be sure, during the fourteenth century the so-called miracle-plays flourished abundantly in England, and were, as there is every reason to believe, already largely performed by the trading-companies of London and the towns. The allusions in Chaucer to these beginnings of our English drama are, however, remarkably scanty. The *Wife of Bath* mentions plays of miracles among the other occasions of religious sensation haunted by her, clad in her gay scarlet gown—including vigils, processions, preachings, pilgrimages, and marriages. And the jolly parish-clerk of the *Miller's Tale*, we are informed, at times, in order to show his lightness and his skill, played " Herod on a scaffold high "—thus, by-the-bye, emulating the parish clerks of London, who are known to have been among the performers of miracles in the Middle Ages. The allusion to Pilate's voice in the *Miller's Prologue*, and that in the *Tale* to

> " The sorrow of Noah with his fellowship
>   That he had ere he got his wife to ship,"

seem likewise dramatic reminiscences; and the occurrence of these three allusions in a single *Tale* and its *Prologue* would incline one to think that Chaucer had recently amused himself at one of these performances. But plays are not mentioned among the entertainments enumerated at the opening of the *Pardoner's Tale;* and it would in

any case have been unlikely that Chaucer should have
paid much attention to diversions which were long chiefly
"visited" by the classes with which he could have no
personal connexion, and even at a much later date were
dissociated in men's minds from poetry and literature.
Had he ever written anything remotely partaking of the
nature of a dramatic piece, it could at the most have been
the words of the songs in some congratulatory royal pa-
geant such as Lydgate probably wrote on the return of
Henry V. after Agincourt; though there is not the least
reason for supposing Chaucer to have taken so much interest in the "ridings" through the City which occupied
many a morning of the idle apprentice of the *Cook's Tale*,
Perkyn Revellour. It is, perhaps, more surprising to find
Chaucer, who was a reader of several Latin poets, and who
had heard of more, both Latin and Greek, show no knowledge whatever of the ancient classical drama, with which
he may accordingly be fairly concluded to have been wholly unacquainted.

To one further aspect of Chaucer's realism as a poet
reference has already been made; but a final mention of
it may most appropriately conclude this sketch of his poetical characteristics. His descriptions of nature are as
true as his sketches of human character; and incidental
touches in him reveal his love of the one as unmistakeably
as his unflagging interest in the study of the other. Even
these May-morning *exordia*, in which he was but following
a fashion—faithfully observed both by the French *trouvères*
and by the English romances translated from their productions, and not forgotten by the author of the earlier
part of the *Roman de la Rose* — always come from his
hands with the freshness of natural truth. They cannot
be called original in conception, and it would be difficult

to point out in them anything strikingly original in execution; yet they cannot be included among those matter-
of-course notices of morning and evening, sunrise and sun-
set, to which so many poets have accustomed us since (be
it said with reverence) Homer himself. In Chaucer these
passages make his page "as fresh as is the month of May."
When he went forth on these April and May mornings, it
was not solely with the intent of composing a roundelay or
a *marguérite ;* but we may be well assured he allowed the
song of the little birds, the perfume of the flowers, and the
fresh verdure of the English landscape, to sink into his
very soul. For nowhere does he seem, and nowhere could
he have been, more open to the influence which he received
into himself, and which in his turn he exercised, and exercises upon others, than when he was in fresh contact with
nature. In this influence lies the secret of his genius; in
his poetry there is *life.*

CHAPTER IV.

EPILOGUE.

THE legacy which Chaucer left to our literature was to fructify in the hands of a long succession of heirs; and it may be said, with little fear of contradiction, that at no time has his fame been fresher and his influence upon our poets—and upon our painters as well as our poets—more perceptible than at the present day. When Gower first put forth his *Confessio Amantis,* we may assume that Chaucer's poetical labours, of the fame of which his brother-poet declared the land to be full, had not yet been crowned by his last and greatest work. As a poet, therefore, Gower in one sense owes less to Chaucer than did many of their successors; though, on the other hand, it may be said with truth that to Chaucer is due the fact that Gower (whose earlier productions were in French and in Latin) ever became a poet at all. The *Confessio Amantis* is no book for all times like the *Canterbury Tales ;* but the conjoined names of Chaucer and Gower added strength to one another in the eyes of the generations ensuing, little anxious as these generations were to distinguish which of the pair was really the first to "garnish our English rude" with the flowers of a new poetic diction and art of verse.

The Lancaster period of our history had its days of

national glōry as well as of national humiliation, and indisputably, as a whole, advanced the growth of the nation towards political manhood.   But it brought with it no golden summer to fulfil the promises of the springtide of our modern poetical literature.   The two poets whose names stand forth from the barren after-season of the earlier half of the fifteenth century, were, both of them, according to their own profession, disciples of Chaucer.   In truth, however, Occleve, the only nameworthy poetical writer of the reign of Henry IV., seems to have been less akin as an author to Chaucer than to Gower, while his principal poem manifestly was, in an even greater degree than the *Confessio Amantis*, a severely learned or, as its author terms it, unbuxom book.   Lydgate, on the other hand, the famous monk of Bury, has in him something of the spirit as well as of the manner of Chaucer, under whose advice he is said to have composed one of his principal poems.   Though a monk, he was no stay-at-home or do-nothing; like him of the *Canterbury Tales*, we may suppose Lydgate to have scorned the maxim that a monk out of his cloister is like a fish out of water; and doubtless many days which he could spare from the instruction of youth at St. Edmund's Bury were spent about the London streets, of the sights and sounds of which he has left us so vivacious a record—a kind of farcical supplement to the *Prologue* of the *Canterbury Tales*.   His literary career, part of which certainly belongs to the reign of Henry V., has some resemblance to Chaucer's, though it is less regular and less consistent with itself; and several of his poems bear more or less distinct traces of Chaucer's influence. The *Troy-book* is not founded on *Troilus and Cressid*, though it is derived from the sources which had fed the original of Chaucer's poem; but the *Temple of Glass* seems to have been an imitation of the *House of Fame*; and the *Story of Thebes* is actually introduced by its author as an additional *Canterbury Tale*, and challenges comparison with the rest of the series into which it asks admittance. Both Occleve and Lydgate enjoyed the patronage of a prince of genius descended from the House, with whose founder Chaucer was so closely connected — Humphrey, Duke of Gloucester. Meanwhile, the sovereign of a neighbouring kingdom was in all probability himself the agent who established the influence of Chaucer as predominant in the literature of his native land. The long though honourable captivity in England of King James I. of Scotland —the best poet among kings and the best king among poets, as he has been antithetically called — was consoled by the study of the "hymns" of his "dear masters, Chaucer and Gower," for the happiness of whose souls he prays at the close of his poem, *The King's Quair*. That most charming of love - allegories, in which the Scottish king sings the story of his captivity and of his deliverance by the sweet messenger of love, not only closely imitates Chaucer in detail, more especially at its opening, but is pervaded by his spirit. Many subsequent Scottish poets imitated Chaucer, and some of them loyally acknowledged their debts to him. Gawin Douglas in his *Palace of Honour*, and Henryson in his *Testament of Cressid* and elsewhere, are followers of the Southern master. The wise and brave Sir David Lyndsay was familiar with his writings ; and he was not only occasionally imitated, but praised with enthusiastic eloquence by William Dunbar, "that darling of the Scottish Muses," whose poetical merits Sir Walter Scott, from some points of view, can hardly be said to have exaggerated, when declaring him to have been "justly raised to a level with Chaucer by every judge of poetry, to whom his obsolete language has not rendered him unintelligible." Dunbar knew that this Scottish language was but a form of that which, as he declared, Chaucer had made to " surmount every terrestrial tongue, as far as midnight is surmounted by a May morning."

Meanwhile, in England, the influence of Chaucer continued to live even during the dreary interval which separates from one another two important epochs of our literary history. Now, as in the days of the Norman kings, ballads orally transmitted were the people's poetry ; and one of these popular ballads carried the story of *Patient Grissel* into regions where Chaucer's name was probably unknown. When, after the close of the troubled season of the Roses, our poetic literature showed the first signs of a revival, they consisted in a return to the old masters of the fourteenth century. The poetry of Hawes, the learned author of the crabbed *Pastime of Pleasure*, exhibits an undeniable continuity with that of Chaucer, Gower, and Lydgate, to which triad he devotes a chapter of panegyric. Hawes, however, presses into the service of his allegory not only all the Virtues and all the Vices, whom from habit we can tolerate in such productions, but also Astronomy, Geometry, Arithmetic, and the rest of the seven Daughters of Doctrine, whom we *cannot*, and is altogether inferior to the least of his models. It is, at the same time, to his credit that he seems painfully aware of his inability to cope with either Chaucer or Lydgate as to vigour of invention. There is, in truth, more of the dramatic spirit of Chaucer in Barklay's *Ship of Fools*, which, though essentially a translation, achieved in England the popularity of an original work ; for this poem, like the *Canterbury Tales*, introduces into its admirable framework a variety of lifelike sketches of character and manners—it has in it that dramatic element which is so Chaucerian a characteristic. But the aim of its author was didactic, which Chaucer's had never been.

When with the poems of Surrey and Wyatt, and with the first attempts in the direction of the regular drama, the opening of the second great age in our literature approached, and when, about half a century afterwards, that age actually opened with an unequalled burst of varied productivity, it would seem as if Chaucer's influence might naturally enough have passed away, or at least become obscured. Such was not, however the case, and Chaucer survived into the age of the English Renascence as an established English classic, in which capacity Caxton had honoured him by twice issuing an edition of his works from the Westminster printing-press. Henry VIII.'s favourite —the reckless but pithy satirist, Skelton—was alive to the merits of his great predecessor; and Skelton's patron, William Thynne, a royal official, busied himself with editing Chaucer's works. The loyal servant of Queen Mary, the wise and witty John Heywood, from whose *Interludes* the step is so short to the first regular English comedy, in one of these pieces freely plagiarised a passage in the *Canterbury Tales*. Tottel, the printer of the favourite poetic *Miscellany* published shortly before Queen Elizabeth's accession, included in his collection the beautiful lines, cited above, called *Good Counsel of Chaucer*. And when at last the Elizabethan era properly so-called began, the proof was speedily given that geniuses worthy of holding fellowship with Chaucer had assimilated into their own literary growth what was congruous to it in his, just as he had assimilated to himself—not always improving, but hardly ever merely borrowing or taking over—much that he had found in the French *trouvères*, and in Italian poetry and prose. The first work which can be included in the great period of Eliza-

9*

bethan literature is the *Shepherd's Calendar*, where Spenser is still in a partly imitative stage; and it is Chaucer whom he imitates and extols in his poem, and whom his *alter ego*, the mysterious "*E. K.*," extols in preface and notes. The longest of the passages in which reference is made by Spenser to Chaucer, under the pseudonym of Tityrus, is more especially noteworthy, both as showing the veneration of the younger for the older poet, and as testifying to the growing popularity of Chaucer at the time when Spenser wrote.

The same great poet's debt to his revered predecessor in the *Daphnaïda* has been already mentioned. The *Fairy Queen* is the masterpiece of an original mind, and its supreme poetic quality is a lofty magnificence upon the whole foreign to Chaucer's genius; but Spenser owed something more than his archaic forms to "Tityrus," with whose style he had erst disclaimed all ambition to match his pastoral pipe. In a well-known passage of his great epos he declares that it is through sweet infusion of the older poet's own spirit that he, the younger, follows the footing of his feet, in order so the rather to meet with his meaning. It was this, the romantic spirit proper, which Spenser sought to catch from Chaucer, but which, like all those who consciously seek after it, he transmuted into a new quality and a new power. With Spenser the change was into something mightier and loftier. He would, we cannot doubt, readily have echoed the judgment of his friend and brother-poet concerning Chaucer. "I know not," writes Sir Philip Sidney, "whether to marvel more, either that he in that misty time could see so clearly, or that we, in this clear age, walk so stumblingly after him. Yet had he," adds Sidney, with the generosity of a true critic, who is not lost in wonder at his own cleverness in discovering defects, "great wants, fit to be forgiven in so reverent an antiquity." And yet a third Elizabethan, Michael Drayton, pure of tone and high of purpose, joins his voice to those of Spenser and Sidney, hailing in the "noble Chaucer"

> ". . . The first of those that ever brake
> Into the Muses' treasure and first spake
> In weighty numbers,"

and placing Gower, with a degree of judgment not reached by his and Chaucer's immediate successors, in his proper relation of poetic rank to his younger but greater contemporary.

To these names should be added that of George Puttenham—if he was indeed the author of the grave and elaborate treatise, dedicated to Lord Burghley, on *The Art of English Poësy*. In this work mention is repeatedly made of Chaucer, "father of our English poets;" and his learning, and "the natural of his pleasant wit," are alike judiciously commended. One of Puttenham's best qualities as a critic is that he never speaks without his book; and he comes very near to discovering Chaucer's greatest gift when noticing his excellence in *prosopographia* — a term which to Chaucer would, perhaps, have seemed to require translation. At the obsoleteness of Chaucer's own diction this critic, who writes entirely "for the better brought-up sort," is obliged to shake his learned head.

Enough has been said in the preceding pages to support the opinion that among the wants which fell to the lot of Chaucer as a poet, perhaps the greatest (though Sidney would never have allowed this) was the want of poetic form most in harmony with his most characteristic gifts. The influence of Chaucer upon the dramatists of the Elizabethan age was probably rather indirect and general than

direct and personal; but indications or illustrations of it
may be traced in a considerable number of these writers,
including, perhaps, among the earliest Richard Edwards
as the author of a non-extant tragedy, *Palamon and Arcite*, and among the latest the author—or authors—of *The
Two Noble Kinsmen*. Besides Fletcher and Shakspeare,
Greene, Nash, and Middleton, and more especially Jonson
(as both poet and grammarian), were acquainted with
Chaucer's writings; so that it is perhaps rather a proof
of the widespread popularity of the *Canterbury Tales*
than the reverse that they were not largely resorted to
for materials by the Elizabethan and Jacobean dramatists.
Under Charles I. *Troilus and Cressid* found a translator
in Sir Francis Kynaston, whom Cartwright congratulated
on having made it possible "that we read Chaucer now
without a dictionary." A personage, however, in Cartwright's best known play, the Antiquary Moth, prefers to
talk on his own account "genuine" Chaucerian English.

To pursue the further traces of the influence of Chaucer through such a literary aftergrowth as the younger
Fletchers, into the early poems of Milton, would be beyond the purpose of the present essay. In the treasure-
house of that great poet's mind were gathered memories
and associations innumerable, though the sublimest flights
of his genius soared aloft into regions whither the imagination of none of our earlier poets had preceded
them. On the other hand, the days have passed for
attention to be spared for the treatment experienced by
Chaucer in the Augustan age, to which he was a barba-
rian only to be tolerated if put into the court-dress of the
final period of civilisation. Still, even thus, he was not
left altogether unread; nor was he in all cases adapted
without a certain measure of success. The irrepressible

vigour, and the frequent felicity, of Dryden's *Fables* contrast advantageously with the tame evenness of the *Temple of Fame*, an early effort by Pope, who had wit enough to imitate in a juvenile parody some of the grossest peculiarities of Chaucer's manner, but who would have been quite ashamed to reproduce him in a serious literary performance, without the inevitable polish and cadence of his own style of verse.   Later modernisations—even of those which a band of poets in some instances singularly qualified for the task put forth in a collection published in the year 1841, and which, on the part of some of them at least, was the result of conscientious endeavour—it is needless to characterise here.   Slight incidental use has been made of some of these in this essay, the author of which would gladly have abstained from printing a single modernised phrase or word—most of all, any which he has himself been guilty of re-casting.   The time cannot be far distant when even the least unsuccessful of such attempts will no longer be accepted, because no such attempts whatever will be any longer required.   No Englishman or Englishwoman need go through a very long or very laborious apprenticeship in order to become able to read, understand, and enjoy what Chaucer himself wrote.   But if this apprenticeship be too hard, then some sort of makeshift must be accepted, or antiquity must remain the "cankerworm" even of a great national poet, as Spenser said it had already in his day proved to be of Chaucer.

Meanwhile, since our poetic literature has long thrown off the shackles which forced it to adhere to one particular group of models, he is not a true English poet who should remain uninfluenced by any of the really great among his predecessors.   If Chaucer has again, in a special sense, become the "master dear and father reverent" of

some of our living poets, in a wider sense he must hold
this relation to them all and to all their successors, so long
as he continues to be known and understood.   As it is,
there are few worthies of our literature whose names seem
to awaken throughout the English-speaking world a readi-
er sentiment of familiar regard; and in New England,
where the earliest great poet of Old England is cherished
not less warmly than among ourselves, a kindly cunning
has thus limned his likeness :—

> "An old man in a lodge within a park;
>   The chamber walls depicted all around
>   With portraiture of huntsman, hawk and hound,
> And the hurt deer.   He listeneth to the lark,
> Whose song comes with the sunshine through the dark
> Of painted glass in leaden lattice bound;
> He listeneth and he laugheth at the sound,
> Then writeth in a book like any clerk.
> He is the poet of the dawn, who wrote
> The Canterbury Tales, and his old age
> Made beautiful with song; and as I read
> I hear the crowing cock, I hear the note
> Of lark and linnet, and from every page
> Rise odours of ploughed field or flowery mead."

GLOSSARY.

Bencite = benedicite.
Clepe, call.
Deem, judge.
Despitous, angry to excess.
Digne, fit ;—disdainful.
Frere, friar.
Gentle, well-born.
Keep, care.
Languor, grief.
Meinie, following, household.
Meet, mate (?), measure (?).
Overthwart, across.
Parage, rank, degree.
Press, crowd.

Rede, advise, counsel.
Reeve, steward, bailiff.
Ruth, pity.
Scall, scab.
Shapely, fit.
Sithe, time.
Spiced, nice, scrupulous.
Targe, target, shield.
Y prefix of past participle as in
  y-bee = *bee*(*n*).
While, time ; *to quite his while*, to
  reward his pains.
Wieldy, active.
Wone, custom, habit.

*** A dotted ë should always be sounded in reading.

THE END.

ENGLISH MEN OF LETTERS.

EDITED BY JOHN MORLEY.

These short Books are addressed to the general public, with a view both to stirring and satisfying an interest in literature and its great topics in the minds of those who have to run as they read. An immense class is growing up, and must every year increase, whose education will have made them alive to the importance of the masters of our literature, and capable of intelligent curiosity as to their performances. The series is intended to give the means of nourishing this curiosity to an extent that shall be copious enough to be profitable for knowledge and life, and yet be brief enough to serve those whose leisure is scanty. The following volumes are now ready:

12mo, Cloth, 75 cents a volume.

VOLUMES IN PREPARATION:

Others will be announced.

PUBLISHED BY HARPER & BROTHERS, NEW YORK.

VALUABLE AND INTERESTING WORKS

FOR

PUBLIC & PRIVATE LIBRARIES,

PUBLISHED BY HARPER & BROTHERS, NEW YORK.

☞ *For a full List of Books suitable for Libraries published by* HARPER & BROTHERS, *see* HARPERS' CATALOGUE, *which may be had gratuitously on application to the Publishers personally, or by letter enclosing Nine Cents in Postage stamps.*

☞ HARPER & BROTHERS *will send their publications by mail, postage prepaid, on receipt of the price.*

MACAULAY'S ENGLAND. The History of England from the Accession of James II. By THOMAS BABINGTON MACAULAY. New Edition, from new Electrotype Plates. 8vo, Cloth, with Paper Labels, Uncut Edges and Gilt Tops, 5 vols. in a Box, $10 00 per set. Sold only in sets. Cheap Edition, 5 vols. in a Box, 12mo, Cloth, $4 00; Sheep, $6 00.

MACAULAY'S LIFE AND LETTERS. The Life and Letters of Lord Macaulay. By his Nephew, G. OTTO TREVELYAN, M.P. With Portrait on Steel. Complete in 2 vols., 8vo, Cloth, Uncut Edges and Gilt Tops, $5 00; Sheep, $6 00; Half Calf, $9 50. Popular Edition, two vols. in one, 12mo, Cloth, $1 75.

HUME'S ENGLAND. The History of England, from the Invasion of Julius Cæsar to the Abdication of James II., 1688. By DAVID HUME. New and Elegant Library Edition, from new Electrotype Plates. 6 vols. in a Box, 8vo, Cloth, with Paper Labels, Uncut Edges and Gilt Tops, $12 00. Sold only in sets. Popular Edition, 6 vols. in a Box, 12mo, Cloth, $4 80; Sheep, $7 20.

GIBBON'S ROME. The History of the Decline and Fall of the Roman Empire. By EDWARD GIBBON. With Notes by Rev. H. H. MILMAN and M. GUIZOT. With Index. 6 vols. in a Box, 12mo, Cloth, $4 80; Sheep, $7 20. *New Edition, from new Electrotype Plates, in Press.*

HILDRETH'S UNITED STATES. History of the United States. FIRST SERIES: From the Discovery of the Continent to the Organization of the Government under the Federal Constitution. SECOND SERIES: From the Adoption of the Federal Constitution to the End of the Sixteenth Congress. By RICHARD HILDRETH. Popular Edition, 6 vols. in a Box, 8vo, Cloth, with Paper Labels, Uncut Edges and Gilt Tops, $12 00. Sold only in sets. (*In Press.*)

MOTLEY'S DUTCH REPUBLIC. The Rise of the Dutch Republic. A History. By JOHN LOTHROP MOTLEY, LL.D., D.C.L. With a Portrait of William of Orange. Cheap Edition, 3 vols. in a Box, 8vo, Cloth, with Paper Labels, Uncut Edges and Gilt Tops, $6 00. Sold only in sets. Original Library Edition, 3 vols., 8vo, Cloth, $10 50; Sheep, $12 00; Half Calf, $17 25.

MOTLEY'S UNITED NETHERLANDS. History of the United Netherlands: from the Death of William the Silent to the Twelve Years' Truce—1609. With a full View of the English-Dutch Struggle against Spain, and of the Origin and Destruction of the Spanish Armada. By JOHN LOTHROP MOTLEY, LL.D., D.C.L. Portraits. Cheap Edition, 4 vols. in a Box, 8vo, Cloth, with Paper Labels, Uncut Edges and Gilt Tops, $8 00. Sold only in sets. Original Library Edition, 4 vols., 8vo, Cloth, $14 00; Sheep, $16 00; Half Calf, $23 00.

MOTLEY'S LIFE AND DEATH OF JOHN OF BARNEVELD. The Life and Death of John of Barneveld, Advocate of Holland: with a View of the Primary Causes and Movements of "The Thirty-years' War." By JOHN LOTHROP MOTLEY, LL.D., D.C.L. Illustrated. Cheap Edition, 2 vols. in a Box, 8vo, Cloth, with Paper Labels, Uncut Edges and Gilt Tops, $4 00. Sold only in sets. Original Library Edition, 2 vols., 8vo, Cloth, $7 00; Sheep, $8 00; Half Calf, $11 50.

BENJAMIN'S CONTEMPORARY ART. Contemporary Art in Europe. By S. G. W. BENJAMIN. Illustrated. 8vo, Cloth, $3 50.

BENJAMIN'S ART IN AMERICA. Art in America. By S. G. W. BENJAMIN. Illustrated. 8vo, Cloth, $4 00.

THE FIRST CENTURY OF THE REPUBLIC. A Review of American Progress. 8vo, Cloth, $5 00.

HUDSON'S HISTORY OF JOURNALISM. Journalism in the United States, from 1690 to 1872. By FREDERIC HUDSON. 8vo, Cloth, $5 00; Half Calf, $7 25.

JEFFERSON'S LIFE. The Domestic Life of Thomas Jefferson: Compiled from Family Letters and Reminiscences, by his Great-granddaughter, SARAH N. RANDOLPH. Illustrated. Crown 8vo, Cloth, $2 50.

SQUIER'S PERU. Peru: Incidents of Travel and Exploration in the Land of the Incas. By E. GEORGE SQUIER, M.A., F.S.A., late U. S. Commissioner to Peru. With Illustrations. 8vo, Cloth, $5 00.

MYERS'S LOST EMPIRES. Remains of Lost Empires: Sketches of the Ruins of Palmyra, Nineveh, Babylon, and Persepolis. By P. V. N. MYERS. Illustrated. 8vo, Cloth, $3 50.

KINGLAKE'S CRIMEAN WAR. The Invasion of the Crimea: its Origin, and an Account of its Progress down to the Death of Lord Raglan. By ALEXANDER WILLIAM KINGLAKE. With Maps and Plans. Three Volumes now ready. 12mo, Cloth, $2 00 per vol.

LAMB'S COMPLETE WORKS. The Works of Charles Lamb. Comprising his Letters, Poems, Essays of Elia, Essays upon Shakspeare, Hogarth, etc., and a Sketch of his Life, with the Final Memorials, by T. NOON TALFOURD. With Portrait. 2 vols., 12mo, Cloth, $3 00.

LAWRENCE'S HISTORICAL STUDIES. Historical Studies. By EUGENE LAWRENCE. Containing the following Essays : The Bishops of Rome.—Leo and Luther.—Loyola and the Jesuits.—Ecumenical Councils.—The Vaudois.—The Huguenots.—The Church of Jerusalem.—Dominic and the Inquisition.—The Conquest of Ireland. —The Greek Church. 8vo, Cloth, Uncut Edges and Gilt Tops, $3 00.

LOSSING'S FIELD-BOOK OF THE REVOLUTION. Pictorial Field-Book of the Revolution : or, Illustrations by Pen and Pencil of the History, Biography, Scenery, Relics, and Traditions of the War for Independence. By BENSON J. LOSSING. 2 vols., 8vo, Cloth, $14 00; Sheep or Roan, $15 00; Half Calf, $18 00.

LOSSING'S FIELD-BOOK OF THE WAR OF 1812. Pictorial Field-Book of the War of 1812: or, Illustrations by Pen and Pencil of the History, Biography, Scenery, Relics, and Traditions of the last War for American Independence. By BENSON J. LOSSING. With several hundred Engravings on Wood by Lossing and Barritt, chiefly from Original Sketches by the Author. 1088 pages, 8vo, Cloth, $7 00; Sheep, $8 50; Roan, $9 00; Half Calf, $10 00.

FORSTER'S LIFE OF DEAN SWIFT. The Early Life of Jonathan Swift (1667–1711). By JOHN FORSTER. With Portrait. 8vo, Cloth, Uncut Edges and Gilt Tops, $2 50.

HALLAM'S MIDDLE AGES. View of the State of Europe during the Middle Ages. By HENRY HALLAM. 8vo, Cloth, $2 00 ; Sheep, $2 50.

HALLAM'S CONSTITUTIONAL HISTORY OF ENGLAND. The Constitutional History of England, from the Accession of Henry VII. to the Death of George II. By HENRY HALLAM. 8vo, Cloth, $2 00; Sheep, $2 50.

HALLAM'S LITERATURE. Introduction to the Literature of Europe during the Fifteenth, Sixteenth, and Seventeenth Centuries. By HENRY HALLAM. 2 vols., 8vo, Cloth, $4 00 ; Sheep, $5 00.

GREEN'S ENGLISH PEOPLE. History of the English People. By JOHN RICHARD GREEN, M.A. 3 volumes ready. 8vo, Cloth, $2 50 per volume.

Valuable Works for Public and Private Libraries.

SCHWEINFURTH'S HEART OF AFRICA. The Heart of Africa. Three Years' Travels and Adventures in the Unexplored Regions of the Centre of Africa—from 1868 to 1871. By Dr. GEORG SCHWEINFURTH. Translated by ELLEN E. FREWER. With an Introduction by WINWOOD READE. Illustrated by about 130 Wood-cuts from Drawings made by the Author, and with two Maps. 2 vols., 8vo, Cloth, $8 00.

M'CLINTOCK & STRONG'S CYCLOPÆDIA. Cyclopædia of Biblical, Theological, and Ecclesiastical Literature. Prepared by the Rev. JOHN M'CLINTOCK, D.D., and JAMES STRONG, S.T.D. 8 vols. now ready. Royal 8vo. Price per vol., Cloth, $5 00; Sheep, $6 00; Half Morocco, $8 00. (Sold by Subscription.)

MOHAMMED AND MOHAMMEDANISM: Lectures Delivered at the Royal Institution of Great Britain in February and March, 1874. By R. BOSWORTH SMITH, M.A., Assistant Master in Harrow School; late Fellow of Trinity College, Oxford. With an Appendix containing Emanuel Deutsch's Article on "Islam." 12mo, Cloth, $1 50.

MOSHEIM'S ECCLESIASTICAL HISTORY, Ancient and Modern; in which the Rise, Progress, and Variation of Church Power are considered in their Connection with the State of Learning and Philosophy, and the Political History of Europe during that Period. Translated, with Notes, etc., by A. MACLAINE, D.D. Continued to 1826, by C. COOTE, LL.D. 2 vols., 8vo, Cloth, $4 00; Sheep, $5 00.

HARPER'S NEW CLASSICAL LIBRARY. Literal Translations. The following volumes are now ready. 12mo, Cloth, $1 50 each.

CÆSAR.—VIRGIL.—SALLUST.—HORACE.—CICERO'S ORATIONS.—CICERO'S OFFICES, etc.—CICERO ON ORATORY AND ORATORS.—TACITUS (2 vols.).—TERENCE.—SOPHOCLES.—JUVENAL.—XENOPHON.—HOMER'S ILIAD.—HOMER'S ODYSSEY.—HERODOTUS.—DEMOSTHENES (2 vols.).—THUCYDIDES.—ÆSCHYLUS.—EURIPIDES (2 vols.).—LIVY (2 vols.).—PLATO [Select Dialogues].

PARTON'S CARICATURE. Caricature and Other Comic Art, in All Times and Many Lands. By JAMES PARTON. With 203 Illustrations. 8vo, Cloth, Uncut Edges and Gilt Tops, $5 00; Half Calf, $7 25.

NICHOLS'S ART EDUCATION. Art Education applied to Industry. By GEORGE WARD NICHOLS. Illustrated. 8vo, Cloth, $4 00; Half Calf, $6 25.

VINCENT'S LAND OF THE WHITE ELEPHANT. The Land of the White Elephant: Sights and Scenes in Southeastern Asia. A Personal Narrative of Travel and Adventure in Farther India, embracing the Countries of Burma, Siam, Cambodia, and Cochin-China (1871–2). By FRANK VINCENT, Jr. Illustrated with Maps, Plans, and Wood-cuts. Crown 8vo, Cloth, $3 50.